P9-ASN-396

DAG
HAMMARSKJÖLD

DAG
HAMMARSKJÖLD

Richard N. Sheldon

CHELSEA HOUSE PUBLISHERS
NEW YORK
NEW HAVEN   PHILADELPHIA

BHZ24Sh

EDITOR-IN-CHIEF: Nancy Toff
EXECUTIVE EDITOR: Remmel T. Nunn
MANAGING EDITOR: Karyn Gullen Browne
COPY CHIEF: Perry Scott King
ART DIRECTOR: Giannella Garrett
PICTURE EDITOR: Elizabeth Terhune

Staff for DAG HAMMARSKJÖLD:

SENIOR EDITOR: John W. Selfridge
ASSISTANT EDITORS: Maria Behan, Pierre Hauser, Kathleen McDermott, Bert Yaeger
COPY EDITORS: Gillian Bucky, Sean Dolan
DESIGN ASSISTANT: Jill Goldreyer
PICTURE RESEARCH: Matthew Miller
LAYOUT: Debby Jay
PRODUCTION COORDINATOR: Alma Rodriguez
COVER ILLUSTRATION: Richard Leonard

CREATIVE DIRECTOR: Harold Steinberg

Frontispiece courtesy of UPI/Bettmann Newsphotos

First Printing

Library of Congress Cataloging in Publication Data

Sheldon, Richard N. DAG HAMMARSKJÖLD

(World leaders past & present)
Bibliography: p.
Includes index.
1. Hammarskjöld, Dag, 1905–1961—Juvenile literature.
2. United Nations—Biography— Juvenile literature. 3.
Statesmen—Biography— Juvenile literature.
[1. Hammarskjöld, Dag, 1905–1961. 2. Statesmen.
3. United Nations—Biography]
I. Title. II. Series.
D839.7.H3S45   1987   341.23′24 [B] [92]   86-31668

ISBN 0-87754-529-4

Contents

CHELSEA HOUSE PUBLISHERS

WORLD LEADERS PAST & PRESENT

ON LEADERSHIP
Arthur M. Schlesinger, jr.

Leadership, it may be said, is really what makes the world go round. Love no doubt smooths the passage; but love is a private transaction between consenting adults. Leadership is a public transaction with history. The idea of leadership affirms the capacity of individuals to move, inspire, and mobilize masses of people so that they act together in pursuit of an end. Sometimes leadership serves good purposes, sometimes bad; but whether the end is benign or evil, great leaders are those men and women who leave their personal stamp on history.

Now, the very concept of leadership implies the proposition that individuals can make a difference. This proposition has never been universally accepted. From classical times to the present day, eminent thinkers have regarded individuals as no more than the agents and pawns of larger forces, whether the gods and goddesses of the ancient world or, in the modern era, race, class, nation, the dialectic, the will of the people, the spirit of the times, history itself. Against such forces, the individual dwindles into insignificance.

So contends the thesis of historical determinism. Tolstoy's great novel *War and Peace* offers a famous statement of the case. Why, Tolstoy asked, did millions of men in the Napoleonic wars, denying their human feelings and their common sense, move back and forth across Europe slaughtering their fellows? "The war," Tolstoy answered, "was bound to happen simply because it was bound to happen." All prior history predetermined it. As for leaders, they, Tolstoy said, "are but the labels that serve to give a name to an end and, like labels, they have the least possible connection with the event." The greater the leader, "the more conspicuous the inevitability and the predestination of every act he commits." The leader, said Tolstoy, is "the slave of history."

Determinism takes many forms. Marxism is the determinism of class. Nazism the determinism of race. But the idea of men and women as the slaves of history runs athwart the deepest human instincts. Rigid determinism abolishes the idea of human freedom—

the assumption of free choice that underlies every move we make, every word we speak, every thought we think. It abolishes the idea of human responsibility, since it is manifestly unfair to reward or punish people for actions that are by definition beyond their control. No one can live consistently by any deterministic creed. The Marxist states prove this themselves by their extreme susceptibility to the cult of leadership.

More than that, history refutes the idea that individuals make no difference. In December 1931 a British politician crossing Park Avenue in New York City between 76th and 77th Streets around 10:30 P.M. looked in the wrong direction and was knocked down by an automobile—a moment, he later recalled, of a man aghast, a world aglare: "I do not understand why I was not broken like an eggshell or squashed like a gooseberry." Fourteen months later an American politician, sitting in an open car in Miami, Florida, was fired on by an assassin; the man beside him was hit. Those who believe that individuals make no difference to history might well ponder whether the next two decades would have been the same had Mario Constasino's car killed Winston Churchill in 1931 and Giuseppe Zangara's bullet killed Franklin Roosevelt in 1933. Suppose, in addition, that Adolf Hitler had been killed in the street fighting during the Munich *Putsch* of 1923 and that Lenin had died of typhus during World War I. What would the 20th century be like now?

For better or for worse, individuals do make a difference. "The notion that a people can run itself and its affairs anonymously," wrote the philosopher William James, "is now well known to be the silliest of absurdities. Mankind does nothing save through initiatives on the part of inventors, great or small, and imitation by the rest of us—these are the sole factors in human progress. Individuals of genius show the way, and set the patterns, which common people then adopt and follow."

Leadership, James suggests, means leadership in thought as well as in action. In the long run, leaders in thought may well make the greater difference to the world. But, as Woodrow Wilson once said, "Those only are leaders of men, in the general eye, who lead in action. . . . It is at their hands that new thought gets its translation into the crude language of deeds." Leaders in thought often invent in solitude and obscurity, leaving to later generations the tasks of imitation. Leaders in action—the leaders portrayed in this series—have to be effective in their own time.

And they cannot be effective by themselves. They must act in response to the rhythms of their age. Their genius must be adapted, in a phrase of William James's, "to the receptivities of the moment." Leaders are useless without followers. "There goes the mob," said the French politician hearing a clamor in the streets. "I am their leader. I must follow them." Great leaders turn the inchoate emotions of the mob to purposes of their own. They seize on the opportunities of their time, the hopes, fears, frustrations, crises, potentialities. They succeed when events have prepared the way for them, when the community is awaiting to be aroused, when they can provide the clarifying and organizing ideas. Leadership ignites the circuit between the individual and the mass and thereby alters history.

It may alter history for better or for worse. Leaders have been responsible for the most extravagant follies and most monstrous crimes that have beset suffering humanity. They have also been vital in such gains as humanity has made in individual freedom, religious and racial tolerance, social justice and respect for human rights.

There is no sure way to tell in advance who is going to lead for good and who for evil. But a glance at the gallery of men and women in *World Leaders—Past and Present* suggests some useful tests.

One test is this: do leaders lead by force or by persuasion? By command or by consent? Through most of history leadership was exercised by the divine right of authority. The duty of followers was to defer and to obey. "Theirs not to reason why,/ Theirs but to do and die." On occasion, as with the so-called "enlightened despots" of the 18th century in Europe, absolutist leadership was animated by humane purposes. More often, absolutism nourished the passion for domination, land, gold and conquest and resulted in tyranny.

The great revolution of modern times has been the revolution of equality. The idea that all people should be equal in their legal condition has undermined the old structure of authority, hierarchy and deference. The revolution of equality has had two contrary effects on the nature of leadership. For equality, as Alexis de Tocqueville pointed out in his great study *Democracy in America*, might mean equality in servitude as well as equality in freedom.

"I know of only two methods of establishing equality in the political world," Tocqueville wrote. "Rights must be given to every citizen, or none at all to anyone . . . save one, who is the master of all." There was no middle ground "between the sovereignty of all and the absolute power of one man." In his astonishing prediction of 20th-century totalitarian dictatorship, Tocqueville explained how the revolution of equality could lead to the *"Führerprinzip"* and more terrible absolutism than the world had ever known.

But when rights are given to every citizen and the sovereignty of all is established, the problem of leadership takes a new form, becomes more exacting than ever before. It is easy to issue commands and enforce them by the rope and the stake, the concentration camp and the *gulag.* It is much harder to use argument and achievement to overcome opposition and win consent. The Founding Fathers of the United States understood the difficulty. They believed that history had given them the opportunity to decide, as Alexander Hamilton wrote in the first Federalist Paper, whether men are indeed capable of basing government on "reflection and choice, or whether they are forever destined to depend . . . on accident and force."

Government by reflection and choice called for a new style of leadership and a new quality of followership. It required leaders to be responsive to popular concerns, and it required followers to be active and informed participants in the process. Democracy does not eliminate emotion from politics; sometimes it fosters demagoguery; but it is confident that, as the greatest of democratic leaders put it, you cannot fool all of the people all of the time. It measures leadership by results and retires those who overreach or falter or fail.

It is true that in the long run despots are measured by results too. But they can postpone the day of judgment, sometimes indefinitely, and in the meantime they can do infinite harm. It is also true that democracy is no guarantee of virtue and intelligence in government, for the voice of the people is not necessarily the voice of God. But democracy, by assuring the right of opposition, offers built-in resistance to the evils inherent in absolutism. As the theologian Reinhold Niebuhr summed it up, "Man's capacity for justice makes democracy possible, but man's inclination to injustice makes democracy necessary."

A second test for leadership is the end for which power is sought. When leaders have as their goal the supremacy of a master race or the promotion of totalitarian revolution or the acquisition and exploitation of colonies or the protection of greed and privilege or the preservation of personal power, it is likely that their leadership will do little to advance the cause of humanity. When their goal is the abolition of slavery, the liberation of women, the enlargement of opportunity for the poor and powerless, the extension of equal rights to racial minorities, the defense of the freedoms of expression and opposition, it is likely that their leadership will increase the sum of human liberty and welfare.

Leaders have done great harm to the world. They have also conferred great benefits. You will find both sorts in this series. Even "good" leaders must be regarded with a certain wariness. Leaders are not demigods; they put on their trousers one leg after another just like ordinary mortals. No leader is infallible, and every leader needs to be reminded of this at regular intervals. Irreverence irritates leaders but is their salvation. Unquestioning submission corrupts leaders and demands followers. Making a cult of a leader is always a mistake. Fortunately hero worship generates its own antidote. "Every hero," said Emerson, "becomes a bore at last."

The signal benefit the great leaders confer is to embolden the rest of us to live according to our own best selves, to be active, insistent, and resolute in affirming our own sense of things. For great leaders attest to the reality of human freedom against the supposed inevitabilities of history. And they attest to the wisdom and power that may lie within the most unlikely of us, which is why Abraham Lincoln remains the supreme example of great leadership. A great leader, said Emerson, exhibits new possibilities to all humanity. "We feed on genius. . . . Great men exist that there may be greater men."

Great leaders, in short, justify themselves by emancipating and empowering their followers. So humanity struggles to master its destiny, remembering with Alexis de Tocqueville: "It is true that around every man a fatal circle is traced beyond which he cannot pass; but within the wide verge of that circle he is powerful and free; as it is with man, so with communities."

1

World Public Servant

A heavy tropical rain was falling in Léopoldville, the capital city of the Republic of the Congo, as a large, black car, tires hissing on the wet pavement, drove away from Patrice Lumumba's house. The former prime minister had been hiding in his own home on the banks of the Congo River since Colonel Joseph Mobutu had taken over the government in a coup three months earlier. Lumumba had many enemies, and it was unsafe for him to go out in Léopoldville. The United Nations, which had sent peacekeeping troops to prevent the outbreak of civil war in this central African nation, had stationed guards outside Lumumba's home to protect him, but Lumumba was still a free man, and when the big, black car sped off through the rainy darkness, the UN troops made no effort to stop it.

Lumumba, chafing under his confinement, had grown restless. On that stormy night in late November 1960 he headed for Port Francqui, in the Congolese province of Kasai, where he had political allies. He was welcomed enthusiastically, and for a few days he enjoyed the role of the great ruler returning to fulfill his destiny of leading his loyal followers to new and glorious triumphs. On December 1, however, Mobutu's men caught up with him. Lu-

> *There is no intellectual activity which more ruthlessly tests the solidity of a man than politics.*
> —DAG HAMMARSKJÖLD

UN Secretary-General Dag Hammarskjöld poses for this 1953 photo with characteristic aplomb. A large part of Hammarskjöld's success in elevating the United Nations to a position of prominence may be attributed to his calm yet forceful presence.

UNITED NATIONS

Never look down to test the ground before taking your next step: only he who keeps his eye fixed on the far horizon will find his right road.

—DAG HAMMARSKJÖLD

Former prime minister of the Congo Patrice Lumumba (right) and former vice-president of the Congolese senate Joseph Okito after their arrest in December 1960 on the orders of the Congo's new leader, Joseph Mobutu, whose military takeover focused attention on the unstable Congolese situation.

mumba was immediately arrested and imprisoned, but even in jail he remained a dangerous rallying point for his followers.

Mobutu decided he had to eliminate his opponent once and for all. The decision, however, necessitated secrecy, for the world was watching closely the turbulent events in the Congo. In February 1961 Mobutu sent Lumumba to the autonomous region of Katanga. He was guarded en route by Baluba tribesmen. The Baluba had been massacred the previous August during military operations ordered by Lumumba. The former prime minister disappeared shortly after his arrival in Katanga.

The safety of Lumumba became the overriding concern of Dag Hammarskjöld, secretary-general of the UN, who months earlier had convinced the UN to send troops to the Congo. Lumumba's arrest had unleashed on the secretary-general a storm of criticism. The Soviet Union had especially harsh words for Hammarskjöld; Lumumba was the strongest pro-Soviet leader in the Congo, and the Soviet Union had hoped to exercise great influence in the country through him. The Soviets now made the accusation that the UN forces in the Congo had aided in Lumumba's arrest and transfer to Katanga. Hammarskjöld, calm yet forceful, continued to demand that the Congo government return Lumumba from Katanga and treat him well and in accordance with due process of law. On February 13 came the terse announcement that Lumumba had died as the result of a brutal beating.

The murder of Lumumba was the last straw for the Soviet Union. The Soviet delegate to the UN, Valerian Zorin, charged Hammarskjöld with direct responsibility in Lumumba's death. Many people believed the Soviet charge and were angry with the secretary-general. A riot broke out at the UN in which 20 unarmed guards were injured. The rioters, using brass knuckles and other weapons, entered the Security Council shouting "Get Hammarskjöld, get Hammarskjöld!" Zorin demanded that the UN pull out of the Congo immediately and

February 1961. A rioter is subdued by UN security guards during a debate on the Congo. Although Hammarskjöld remained neutral throughout the crisis, his policy was denounced as a failure when Lumumba was executed by Mobutu's men.

called for the resignation of the secretary-general. Hammarskjöld prepared to meet his greatest challenge. No one could have predicted that it would also be his last.

Uppsala, the ancient Viking capital of Sweden, is dominated by a huge, red castle and the 400-foot-high spires of a great Gothic cathedral, the largest church in Sweden. As these two structures dominate the city, so they also dominated Dag Hammarskjöld's life as a boy and a young man. The 16th-century red castle, once the residence of the Swedish kings, was his boyhood home. Like a fortress, with two huge towers at each end, it was a fascinating place for an imaginative child. One of the huge meeting rooms served as a playroom, and young Hammarskjöld often led his friends on exciting chases through the maze of dark, mysterious passages that twisted through the castle to the old dungeons deep inside. The towering Lutheran cathedral served as a focal point, a unifying force for the Hammarskjölds, a deeply religious family.

For almost 300 years, since 1610, the Hammarskjölds had served the king, either as soldiers or government administrators. The family name (pronounced "hammarshuld") means "hammer-shield." Hammarskjöld's father, Hjalmar, began his career as a university professor, later carrying on the family tradition by working for the government in several important posts.

The youngest of four sons, Dag Hammarskjöld was born on July 29, 1905, in Jönköping, a town in south-central Sweden. Dag was a young boy when his father became governor of the district of Uppland and the family moved into Vasa castle in Uppsala. Hjalmar, a dignified, stern man, was president of the Bible Society. His wife, Agnes Almquist Hammarskjöld, attended services at the cathedral every Sunday. They were close friends of Archbishop Nathan Söderblom, and young Hammarskjöld and the archbishop's son, Jan, were playmates. As a boy Hammarskjöld developed a powerful sense of personal religion, which remained with him throughout his life.

Hammarskjöld as a youth in the ancient Viking city of Uppsala, Sweden. He was born on July 29, 1905, to a family with a long tradition of service to the Swedish government.

Hjalmar Hammarskjöld, Dag's influential father. During a long career as a public servant, Hjalmar served as district governor, representative to the League of Nations, member of the Swedish parliament, and prime minister from 1914 to 1917.

Young Hammarskjöld was devoted to his mother. A childhood friend said that Agnes "was exactly what the father was not. He was a forbidding figure, authoritative to the point of being rude. She was exuberantly forthcoming . . . with good will and friendliness towards everybody around her." Her personality, in some ways, rubbed off on Hammarskjöld, and he developed a great ability to charm people.

Although Hammarskjöld's childhood was a relatively happy one, he sometimes felt lonely and isolated. Even at a young age, Dag knew he was expected to achieve great success and live up to the family name, but he did not yet know exactly where he fit in or what direction he should take. His brothers Bo and Åke were many years older than Dag. Åke, especially, was a gifted student, and both brothers seemed well on their way to fulfilling the Hammarskjöld tradition of distinguished public careers. Sten was only five years older than Dag, but he was a sickly child, unable to provide much active companionship for his younger brother.

In 1914, when Hammarskjöld was nine years old, his father became prime minister of Sweden — the leader of the nation. At the time Europe was descending into the nightmare of World War I. Hjalmar proclaimed a policy of neutrality for Sweden, which

> *Let the inner take precedence over the outer, the soul over the world, wherever this may lead you.*
> —DAG HAMMARSKJÖLD

AP/WIDE WORLD PHOTOS

Hammarskjöld takes a vacation on the North Sea island of Marstrand during school holiday recess. Even as a young boy Hammarskjöld showed a passion for nature and the outdoors.

meant that the country would stay out of the war and preserve the principles of freedom and justice which were being trampled underfoot by the carnage in the rest of the continent. His policy of holding Sweden out of the conflict, in the belief that principles of international law should govern the conduct of the world's nations, strongly influenced his sons. It also set a precedent for the future leaders of Sweden, who saw the wisdom of the elder Hammarskjöld's policy. Sweden would also remain neutral during World War II, thus avoiding the wholesale destruction suffered by most European countries. Young Hammarskjöld learned well the lesson of neutrality — to avoid taking sides, to remain above any struggle, and to be guided only by principles of fairness and justice.

Hammarskjöld was an outstanding student, the brightest boy in his class. He excelled in mathematics, literature, and languages. Indeed, Hammarskjöld would eventually speak fluent English, French, and German. But the achievements of his father and his older brothers kept him from getting overconfident. When he showed his father his excellent examination scores for entering the University of Uppsala, his father simply told him that one of his brothers, Åke, had done better.

As a university student, Hammarskjöld worked hard. At Uppsala, he earned his first degree in literature and philosophy in only two years, at age 19. Yet it did not impress his father, who had been awarded a degree at 18. Hammarskjöld went on to take graduate degrees in law and economics.

From local Swedish politics to South American poetry, conversations in the Hammarskjöld household always reflected the tremendous intellectual energies of father and son. Hammarskjöld had long talks with Hjalmar on disarmament and international relations. Imbued with a desire to live up to his father's expectations and contribute to the political life of his country, Hammarskjöld absorbed information from many disciplines. He was a voracious reader, familiar with the great works of literature, politics, and economics. He read such well-known authors as Thomas Mann and Hermann

Dag (second from left), age 15, seated with his brothers (left to right) Bo, Åke, and Sten. The competition among the boys for their illustrious father's recognition was fierce.

Hesse, and on long walks with fellow students he would discuss Freudian psychology and Marxist theory.

While at the university, Hammarskjöld reportedly became involved for a short time with the daughter of a respected local family. Nothing came of the romance, however, and Hammarskjöld would never marry. As UN secretary-general, he would remember how his mother had suffered from the absence of his politically active father, and he felt that his busy life prevented him from making a good marriage. He often quipped that bachelorhood should be a prerequisite for the position of secretary-general.

In 1930 the Hammarskjölds moved to the capital city of Stockholm, where Dag enrolled in the University of Stockholm. At the university he completed his graduate program in economics and received his doctorate in 1933. He then began working as an economist with the Swedish government. He impressed his coworkers with his knowledge and dedication, and promotions came quickly. In early 1931 Hammarskjöld had met Sweden's minister of finance, Ernst Wigforss. Wigforss, one of the founders of modern Swedish socialism, had immediately recognized Hammarskjöld's abilities. In 1936 Wigforss appointed him undersecretary of finance. Just 30 years old, Hammarskjöld was the youngest man

If I were as gifted as Dag and had his talent for dealing with people, I should have gone far.
—HJALMAR HAMMARSKJÖLD
Dag's father and Sweden's prime minister

Shoppers stroll through a cobblestoned district in Sweden's capital city of Stockholm. Due to the policy of neutrality originally instituted by Prime Minister Hjalmar Hammarskjöld during World War I, Sweden remained untouched by the ravages of both world wars.

ever to hold that position, and he quickly earned a reputation as one of the most competent and hardworking civil servants in the government. Though Hammarskjöld was attracted by Wigforss's socialist economic ideas, he remained independent of party affiliations, preferring to render his services to his country as a whole rather than to the government in power at the time.

When World War II erupted in 1939, Sweden declared itself officially neutral. Hammarskjöld and other Swedish officials, however, worked secretly to help the Allies — Great Britain, France, and later the Soviet Union and the United States — and particularly Norway, which fell to the Nazis in 1940. When Hammarskjöld became chairman of the national bank of Sweden in 1941 he was in a position to provide financial assistance to the Norwegian government-in-exile in London, often making the risky flight from Sweden to England through skies controlled by the German *Luftwaffe* (air force). After the war, the Norwegian government awarded him one of its highest honors for his aid.

World War II devastated most of the nations of Europe. When the war ended in 1945 Hammarskjöld worked on the complicated problems of reconstructing the European economic and monetary systems. By 1948 he had resigned his positions in the finance ministry and the national bank to devote his time, as head of the Swedish delegation, to the talks being held in France on economic aid to postwar Europe. As a member of the executive committee of the Organization for European Economic Cooperation (OEEC), the group that was setting the foundations for European economic alliances, Hammarskjöld worked in Paris with economists and other experts from all over the world. His command of foreign languages helped make him an able diplomat, while his hard work and powerful intelligence won him many admirers.

During his work with the OEEC, Hammarskjöld was appointed an adviser to the Swedish Ministry of Foreign Affairs. Shortly thereafter, in 1951, he became the vice-minister for foreign affairs. His first diplomatic crisis arose the following year. On vacation in northern Sweden in the summer of 1952, Hammarskjöld received word that a Swedish plane had been shot down over the Baltic Sea by the Soviet Union. A plane that was sent out to search for survivors was also shot down. The foreign minister was on vacation in Italy, so Hammarskjöld, as the next in command, had to handle the protest to the Soviet Union. Still wearing boots and carrying a backpack, Hammarskjöld went straight from the Stockholm airport to his office. The situation was explosive. Such an unprovoked attack could lead to war.

It was up to Hammarskjöld to defuse the situation. For several days he kept up a lively correspondence with the Soviet government. The Soviet messages were always delivered late at night, in time to be published in the morning newspapers, but too late for a Swedish reply to be published at the same time. Thus the Soviet version of events would go unchallenged for a full day. So Hammarskjöld simply kept his office open late so he could write a reply

> *Dag has such purity of character and an intelligence of such a high order that I do not for a moment hesitate to write that he will be Swedish prime minister at a young age.*
> —SVEN STOLPE
> Swedish novelist

as soon as the Soviet note was received and have the morning newspapers carry both. Through careful diplomacy, he was able to satisfy both the Soviet Union and Sweden in working out a peaceful settlement. The Soviet leaders remembered this when they voted for him for secretary-general less than a year later.

Hammarskjöld had the ability to work long hours yet always appear fresh and energetic. He seldom tired. He developed this extraordinary working pattern early in his career in Sweden. He would leave work at six in the evening and have dinner at home with his parents, sometimes stopping to buy flowers for his mother on the way. At nine he would return to his office. If the work load was particularly heavy, he might be joined there by others, to work until about eleven. Then they would all go off to a restaurant, where they would drink tea or coffee and talk about literature, art, or philosophy for an hour. Thus refreshed, they would return to work for several more hours.

Hammarskjöld calmly receives the news of his election as the secretary-general of the UN at his Stockholm office in the spring of 1953. Hammarskjöld proved acceptable to the major powers because he was an experienced diplomat from a small neutral country.

UPI/BETTMANN NEWSPHOTOS

To rest from his demanding work, Hammarskjöld often went hiking and skiing in the mountains. He was greatly interested in nature and the outdoors and served as president of the Swedish Alpinist Club and vice-president of the Swedish Tourist Association.

Hammarskjöld's long hours were well known in Sweden. His hard work had helped shape the policies for a planned economy, the basis of modern Sweden's social program. His efforts in international economics after the end of World War II promoted Western Europe's recovery from the ravages of the war and enhanced his reputation in the international community as a forceful thinker and leader.

Thus it did not surprise anyone, except perhaps Hammarskjöld himself, when, on March 31, 1953, the UN Security Council offered the position of secretary-general, the highest post at the UN, to Dag Hammarskjöld. As he assessed the difficulties that he knew were ahead, Hammarskjöld, like a good mountain climber, was confident of overcoming all obstacles on the way to the difficult summit of international cooperation and world peace. But it would be the hardest climb of his life.

Trygve Lie, the outgoing UN secretary-general, greets Hammarskjöld as he disembarks from an airplane in New York on April 9, 1953. Hammarskjöld's leadership brought about a tremendous increase in the power and influence of the United Nations.

2

"The Most Impossible Job on This Earth"

Towering over the East River in New York City, the UN Secretariat building dwarfs the General Assembly building crouching below it. Occupying the top floor of the massive glass and steel structure is the suite of offices for the secretary-general and his assistants.

In the General Assembly building, the emblem of the United Nations decorates the wall behind the podium in the vast assembly hall. Shining into the room through the skylight in the domed ceiling, a bright shaft of daylight illuminates the rows of blue upholstered chairs and the many green leather-topped desks of light wood. On the podium, the secretary-general sits behind a high, green marble desk. Below is the speaker's rostrum with its microphones. Along the side walls, interpreters in glass booths translate the speaker's words into six official languages, and television cameras record every word and movement.

The United Nations has its roots in World War I. At the end of the war, in 1918, U.S. President Woodrow Wilson proposed the establishment of a League of Nations as a forum in which the countries of the

> *The private man should disappear and the international public servant take his place.*
> —DAG HAMMARSKJÖLD
> after becoming secretary-general of the UN

Hammarskjöld in April 1953, shortly after arriving at the United Nations. In his internal UN policies and his international diplomacy, Hammarskjöld redefined the position of secretary-general.

world could peacefully discuss issues, problems, and needs. It was hoped that such a body would prevent the kind of devastating warfare that Europe had just experienced. The main principles behind the league included nonintervention by one nation in the internal affairs of another; self-determination, whereby the people of a country had the right to decide on their status as a nation; and human rights and individual freedom for everyone.

However, the league soon degenerated due to internal dissension and attempts at domination by the world powers. As Europeans nervously watched the growing power of Adolf Hitler's Nazi Germany and Benito Mussolini's Fascist Italy, it became clear that the league had failed dismally. But the idea that such an organization could still work, improving international relations by substituting words for weapons, never disappeared.

In April 1945, as World War II was ending, delegates from 50 nations met in San Francisco and wrote a formal plan for a new world peacekeeping organization — the United Nations. Member nations would send representatives to discuss international problems. The United States offered the new organization a home in New York City, eventually constructing the UN buildings on Manhattan's East Side. On October 24, 1945, with the ratification of the UN Charter by a majority of the nations involved, a new experiment in international cooperation had begun. By the 1980s more than 100 nations had joined the original 50.

The UN contains six major bodies: Security Coun-

Firebombed Dresden, Germany, lies in ruins after World War II. The United Nations was conceived as an international forum for world grievances, in the hope that the devastation wrought by the two world wars could be avoided in the future.

V. K. Wellington Koo, chairman of the Chinese delegation, is the first representative to sign the UN Charter on June 28, 1945. The United Nations was officially established in October 1945, once the charter was ratified by a majority of the signatory nations.

cil, Secretariat, General Assembly, Economic and Social Council (ECOSOC), Trusteeship Council, and International Court of Justice. The Security Council is the central force of the UN. It deals with the volatile issues of international relations, including disarmament, and its responsibility lies in finding peaceful solutions to problems that arise among nations. The Security Council is also responsible for nominating the secretary-general.

The secretary-general is the chief administrative and executive officer of the UN. He heads the Secretariat, which essentially runs the daily business of the UN. The secretary-general is assisted by a staff of international administrators and, as head of the UN, must communicate with all the member nations.

In the General Assembly, the largest UN body, sit representatives from all the member nations. The assembly is a forum for discussion and, often, argument on world issues. It supervises the ECOSOC, which handles economic and social needs around the world, and the Trusteeship Council, established to aid former colonies in their transition to statehood. The assembly also oversees the numerous smaller, specialized agencies that have multiplied in the UN, including such autonomous bodies as the UN Educational, Scientific, and Cultural Organization (UNESCO), the World Health Organization

A window cleaner works on the UN Secretariat building. The domed General Assembly building, still under construction, stands below. The United States provided a home for the UN in New York City, where all but one of the major UN bodies are located.

One of the main goals of the UN is worldwide sharing of information and resources. This photo collage, published by the UN, demonstrates the progress made possible by international cooperation.

(WHO), and the International Bank for Reconstruction and Development (World Bank).

The only major body that does not meet in New York is the International Court of Justice, which sits at The Hague in the Netherlands. The court renders decisions on disputes among nations that, although not legally binding, are based on international legal agreements that most nations wish to observe.

Late in 1952 the first UN secretary-general, Trygve Lie of Norway, suddenly decided to step down and let someone else lead the organization. Under the UN Charter the five permanent members of the Security Council — at that time, the United States, Great Britain, Republic of China (Taiwan), France, and the Soviet Union — must vote unanimously on all substantive issues. Therefore all five permanent members had to approve the new secretary-general. The permanent members were the strongest nations in the world; therefore, each was unwilling to yield any advantage to the other in the UN. Only someone from a small, neutral country would be acceptable to all.

On that cold spring evening in 1953, the eve of April Fool's Day, Dag Hammarskjöld was convinced his nomination as UN secretary-general was a joke. But the news was soon confirmed, and a week later Trygve Lie met Hammarskjöld at the New York airport with the words, "Welcome to the most impossible job on this earth."

In his first few days as secretary-general, Hammarskjöld went through the United Nations buildings and shook hands with every UN employee, nearly 4,000 of them. The retiring Swede seemed to them a shy and unspectacular bureaucrat. They wondered how he could possibly handle the job of secretary-general. When he had finished all the handshaking, the chief security officer, who had accompanied him during the five days it took to complete the task, blurted out, "God help you, Mr. Secretary-General!"

At the time Hammarskjöld took over at the UN, the employees' morale was low. UN prestige around the world was declining, and its influence was weak. The new secretary-general believed that the strength of the organization rested on the honesty and impartiality of the administrative staff, so he

Next to General Assembly President Lester Pearson of Canada (center) and Assistant Secretary-General André Cordier of France (right), Hammarskjöld, who initially seemed a rather uninspiring leader, takes his seat on the UN rostrum on April 10, 1953.

AP/WIDE WORLD PHOTOS

Issued on July 7, 1950, in Spanish, French, and English, this UN resolution recommended the formation of an international army to counter North Korean aggression toward South Korea. In 1953 the UN arranged an armistice to bring about an end to the conflict.

tightened the employee rules of conduct and reorganized the staff in order to make it more efficient and responsive. He fought against outside influence and pressure. "My first job is to run this house," he told reporters.

One of the most pressing problems Hammarskjöld had to face immediately was the demoralizing interference by the U.S. government into UN affairs. In the postwar years and through the 1950s the United States and the Soviet Union engaged in what has been termed the Cold War. Each nation felt its own security, prestige, and power threatened by what it perceived as the other's determination to dominate the world. In the United States, cold war paranoia was reflected in the government's obsession with communism. Many U.S. citizens were persecuted because of real or imagined affiliations with the Communist party. In what Hammarskjöld called "a short nightmare," the United States tried to tell the UN that some Americans working for the organization were communists and not loyal to the United States. Hammarskjöld informed the United States that according to the UN Charter, it had no right to interfere with the hiring policies of the organization. Furthermore, it had no right to send agents from the Federal Bureau of Investigation (FBI) into the UN buildings to investigate UN employees. Hammarskjöld told American officials that they could submit factual information regarding American employees to him, but it was entirely up to him as secretary-general to decide who could work for the UN. The UN Charter stipulated that all staff employees must first be loyal to the organization in order to maintain the impartiality necessary to mediate international relations. When a staff member was accused of wrongdoing, Hammarskjöld wanted to be able to say, "We have a judicial process — no anonymous testimony, no evidence that doesn't stand up in a court of law." American officials were angry with Hammarskjöld for defying them, but they realized he was right. They did not interfere with his employees again, and they ordered the FBI to stay out of the UN buildings.

Hammarskjöld's streamlining of the UN staff and its functions, his success in stopping outside interference, and his smooth handling of his first UN General Assembly meeting in December 1953 (at which his reorganization plan was overwhelmingly approved) soon convinced everyone that they had underestimated the quiet Swedish economist. A British observer remarked, "It is a tribute to Mr. Hammarskjöld's standing with governments and to his forceful intelligence and diplomatic skill that in less than one year he has got the Assembly's full support."

Hammarskjöld's first international challenge came as a result of the Korean War, which had begun in 1950 when the North Koreans, backed by the communist People's Republic of China, had invaded South Korea. At the urging of the United States, the UN had sent an international army to aid South Korea, with the entire operation under the supervision of the U.S. command there. By 1953 the fighting had reached a stalemate, and the Gen-

The skeptics among us — and non-skeptics are short-lived in the diplomatic thicket — smiled at all this. We had heard such diamond-studded words before. . . . It was not realized at all that the new secretary-general meant every word he said.
—EMERY KELEN
UN staff member and Hammarskjöld's biographer, on Hammarskjöld's early speeches

eral Assembly arranged an armistice pending final peace talks to end the conflict. But at the time of the Geneva peace talks in June 1954, the communist Chinese continued to hold several American airmen as prisoners. The American people were upset and angry that these prisoners had not yet been released. The U.S. government told Hammarskjöld that it had been unable to persuade China to release the airmen and asked the secretary-general for his help. Hammarskjöld decided to go to China and talk to the Chinese leaders himself.

The communist Chinese government, which had only come to power five years earlier, allowed very few foreigners into the country. But its leaders were intrigued by Hammarskjöld's direct approach and agreed to meet with him in Beijing, the capital city of China. Hammarskjöld's strategy was risky, as it marked the first time a UN secretary-general had personally conducted negotiations with a foreign nation. Henry Cabot Lodge, the U.S. ambassador to the UN, declared that the secretary-general was putting "his life's reputation as a diplomat on the chopping block." He could not afford to fail.

A bitterly cold January wind blew over Beijing when Hammarskjöld arrived there. His hosts took him to the Forbidden City, the name for the group of government buildings that once made up the imperial palace. The Chinese treated him to exotic dinners and receptions in such places as the Palace of Purple Light. They took him on trips to see the Painted Gallery at the summer palace, the great Ming dynasty tombs, the gilded Hall of Supreme Harmony, the Gate of Heavenly Peace, and the Temple of Heaven. On these tours Hammarskjöld, walking "at a terrific pace," left his UN aides panting breathlessly behind. In a palace called the Hall of Western Flowers, within the Forbidden City, Hammarskjöld and the Chinese leader Zhou Enlai carried on their discussions for several days.

The negotiations were awkward because the People's Republic of China was not a member of the UN; the Nationalist government of Chiang Kai-shek, which had fled to Taiwan after the communist revolution, was still recognized at the UN as the official

Chinese government. In addition, the General Assembly resolution authorizing Hammarskjöld to go to China was expressed in language the Chinese found insulting. So Hammarskjöld never mentioned the resolution to them, simply explaining that he had the power to represent the UN and to discuss international problems. The discussion between Zhou and Hammarskjöld covered a wide range of topics. Besides the prisoner problem, they discussed China's desire for membership in the UN, as well as such subjects as philosophy, literature, politics, and history. Hammarskjöld impressed his hosts with his knowledge of China's history and culture.

In a private letter, Hammarskjöld later wrote that "the journey to China was a fantastic experience." He described Zhou Enlai as a man "with a heart of steel, bloody hands, stern self-control, and a very warm smile."

When he left China Hammarskjöld had no prom-

In December 1954 Hammarskjöld leaves for the People's Republic of China in an effort to free U.S. airmen still held there from the Korean War. Hammarskjöld was the first secretary-general to personally conduct such delicate diplomatic talks.

ises from the Chinese, yet he was optimistic. The Chinese were very proud and did not want to give the world the impression that they had yielded to pressure. Hammarskjöld figured it would take them about six months to release the prisoners, but he could not express his hopeful feelings for fear of alienating the Chinese. Reporters clamored for news when he returned from his trip. He would only say that the talks were useful.

In Sweden, a Chinese diplomat learned from one of Hammarskjöld's friends that the secretary-general would be in Sweden to celebrate his 50th birthday in July 1955. He asked what Hammarskjöld would like for a birthday gift and was told that the release of the American airmen would be the best present.

Late in July Hammarskjöld arrived at his beach house in southern Sweden. On his birthday Hammarskjöld and some friends went out early in the morning on a fishing boat. When they returned to shore at sunset, the beach and hills were alive with reporters, photographers, and curious people who had come to get a story or congratulate the secretary-general on his birthday. Hammarskjöld spoke with them very briefly, then hurried straight to his house. There he found a pile of letters, among them

Premier Zhou Enlai of the People's Republic of China meets with Hammarskjöld to discuss the release of the captive U.S. airmen. Hammarskjöld's diplomacy bore fruit in July 1955 when the Americans were unconditionally freed.

UPI/BETTMANN NEWSPHOTOS

a telegram from Zhou Enlai. The Chinese leader wished Hammarskjöld a happy birthday — China was releasing the American airmen. The unassuming secretary-general was, from that moment forward, recognized by the world as one of its most effective leaders.

Hammarskjöld's efforts in his first years at the UN were not all successful. When the U.S. government secretly sponsored a coup in the Central American nation of Guatemala in 1954, Hammarskjöld, in attempting to bring the situation into open discussion in the UN, found himself blocked on all sides by the U.S. delegates and their allies. The incident, however, provided Hammarskjöld with a valuable lesson in dealing with a superpower nation that was intent on pursuing its own course despite the terms of the UN Charter. It also made him more certain that the UN was the only real hope for the smaller nations of the world.

Six of the released American airmen stand with native Hawaiian beauty queens after their release from China in the summer of 1955. Hammarskjöld's success in bringing these men home boosted his prestige as an international diplomat.

3

Israel and the Arabs

The trip to China was only the first of many diplomatic trips Hammarskjöld made as secretary-general of the UN. In early 1956 he traveled around the world to meet the leaders of many of the countries that were members of the UN. He returned from this trip greatly concerned about the likelihood of war in the Middle East.

Suspicion, hatred, violence, and terrorism — these had been daily facts of life for Jews and Arabs in the Middle East for many years. In a worldwide movement to return to the homeland that was theirs in biblical times, Jews had begun moving to Palestine, a small country on the eastern Mediterranean shore, over 50 years earlier. At first the flow of people into the area was only a trickle. But by the 1930s and 1940s it had become a flood, as many Jews fled the war in Europe and the death camps set up by Hitler to destroy them as a people.

The Arabs who already lived in Palestine and considered it an Arab land resented this influx of foreigners, and some of them responded by terrorizing the Jewish settlements. Great Britain, which had administered Palestine under the terms of a League of Nations mandate since shortly after the end of World War I, decided to relinquish the mandate and

Since wars begin in the minds of men, it is in the minds of men that the defenses of peace must be constructed.
—from the constitution of the United Nations Educational, Scientific and Cultural Organization

Secretary-General Hammarskjöld sits at his desk in his UN office in the early 1950s. During these years Hammarskjöld was deeply concerned about peace in the Middle East and devoted a great deal of his time and effort to the troubled area.

The emblem of the United Nations depicts the world's continents surrounded by an olive wreath, the traditional symbol of peace. The words "We Believe" reflect conviction in the organization's peacekeeping mission, which was sorely tested by the Middle East conflicts.

refer the matter to the UN, which voted to create two separate states, one Arab and one Jewish. The UN member states hoped that this action would bring at least a temporary peace to the area while they sought a more permanent solution. But the Palestinian Arabs, as well as many of the neighboring Arab states, felt cheated and refused to accept the UN decision. Local fighting became more common. Within a few months the Jews had gained the upper hand, driving the Arabs from much of the territory they had been inhabiting, even taking some of the land allotted by the UN partition to the Arabs.

In early 1948 the British government withdrew its troops, in accordance with the timetable it had established with the UN. When the Jews proclaimed the creation of their own nation — Israel — in May 1948, Lebanon, Syria, Egypt, Iraq, and Jordan declared war on the new state. The Arabs were confident that the Israelis could not stand up to the might of five Arab armies.

But Israel proved to be a tough opponent, and when the UN requested an armistice at the end of 1948 it was accepted by both sides. Israel had gained even more territory in the war. What remained of the area that was supposed to form a Palestine Arab state was taken over by Jordan.

As a result of these wars many Arabs, referred to as Palestinians, were uprooted from their homeland. Unwanted and viewed with mistrust in Israel, they wandered the Middle East as homeless refugees. Thousands streamed into Jordan and Lebanon, putting a severe strain on the economies of these nations. By the time Hammarskjöld took over as UN secretary-general, there were nearly a million Palestinian refugees living in special camps scattered among the Arab nations. Resented by other Arabs as competitors for a limited number of jobs, huddled in special camps with limited food, clothing, and medical facilities, these refugees posed a serious and immediate problem for several Middle Eastern governments.

The UN-engineered Israel-Egypt armistice agreement had established a demilitarized zone at the

UPI/BETTMANN NEWSPHOTOS

A Palestinian boy cares for his sister at a refugee camp in Lebanon. When thousands of Arabs fled the newly created state of Israel in 1948, the UN attempted to alleviate their plight by providing them with food, clothes, and shelter.

border town of El Auja. The UN armistice between the Arabs and Israelis was shaky, however, and was unable to prevent Palestinian guerrilla attacks and Israeli counterattacks across the UN demarcation line. For several years a small UN truce supervisory section oversaw the uneasy peace. By 1956, however, both countries had violated the armistice, building up military forces along their respective borders. The beleaguered Israeli leader, David Ben-Gurion, gave up hope that the UN could break the bloody deadlock and come up with a long-range solution. He proclaimed a policy of aggressive retaliation, stating that Israel would deliver "two blows for one" against the Arabs.

On a preliminary visit to the Middle East in January 1956, Hammarskjöld talked with Ben-Gurion and Gamal Abdel Nasser, president of Egypt. The secretary-general found the situation explosive; all-out war seemed imminent. The UN Security Council voted to send Hammarskjöld back to the Middle East in a last desperate attempt to prevent more bloodshed.

Using Beirut, the capital of Lebanon, as a headquarters, Hammarskjöld spent the month of April in a "diplomatic marathon," shuttling back and forth between the capital cities of Egypt, Israel, Syria, and Jordan. The negotiations were slow and frustrating. Hammarskjöld had to overcome the deep hatred between the Arabs and the Israelis as well as their suspicion of him. Each side thought the secretary-general secretly favored the other. The friendship that developed between Hammarskjöld

Hammarskjöld tours a Palestinian refugee camp near Beirut, Lebanon, in 1956. When he became secretary-general, almost 1 million Palestinians lived in refugee camps in several Arab nations, a situation he feared would eventually explode if not remedied.

and Egyptian Foreign Minister Mahmoud Fawzi, with whom Hammarskjöld shared a deep interest in literature and philosophy, led the British and French to suspect that Hammarskjöld was biased in favor of Egypt.

Nasser had come to power in Egypt through a revolution in 1952. A former army colonel, he had little political or diplomatic experience, but his fiery Arab nationalism proved extremely popular with Arabs not only in Egypt but throughout the Middle East. He had great charm and a burning ambition to make Egypt the dominant Middle Eastern power.

At first Nasser misjudged Hammarskjöld. Once, in the early stages of the discussions, Nasser seemed to give him assurances on an important point, but

From the right: Hammarskjöld, Israeli Prime Minister David Ben-Gurion, and Israeli Foreign Minister Moshe Sharett meet in Israel during the secretary-general's 1956 tour of the Middle East. Ben-Gurion and Hammarskjöld developed a deep mutual respect.

just before Hammarskjöld boarded a plane to leave Cairo he was handed a document stating that Nasser would not hold to the understanding. Hammarskjöld drove straight back to Nasser's office and demanded an immediate meeting with the president. He then told Nasser that he would never agree to the mere appearance of an understanding. Nasser backed down and gave Hammarskjöld a genuine agreement.

Hammarskjöld held long and involved discussions with the Israeli leader, David Ben-Gurion. Straightforward and blunt, Ben-Gurion often disagreed violently with Hammarskjöld, but each respected the other's intelligence. Ben-Gurion was impressed with Hammarskjöld's knowledge of the Middle East and came to appreciate the secretary-general's skill at negotiating.

By the time Hammarskjöld returned to New York in May, he had won the trust of both Nasser and

Egyptian President Gamal Abdel Nasser (right) met with Hammarskjöld in April and November 1956 to discuss the critical situation in the Middle East. Hammarskjöld's commitment to a just solution to the conflict impressed the Arab leader.

UNITED NATIONS

Ben-Gurion and somehow managed to secure written agreements from Egypt, Israel, Lebanon, Jordan, and Syria for a cease-fire. An Israeli report summed up the secretary-general's achievement: "For the first time in fact since the partition resolution of 1947 the stock of the United Nations in the Middle East stands higher than that of any of the great powers in the eyes of the Arabs and of the Israelis. This has happened not as a result of any kind of appeasement or mediation, but simply as a consequence of the rigid honesty of purpose displayed by the secretary-general and the cooperation which it has won for him from the two premiers who mattered — Nasser and Ben-Gurion." But Hammarskjöld's fight to preserve peace in the Middle East was far from over.

Hammarskjöld (in sunglasses) surveys the ruins of the war-torn Ramat Rachel settlement outside Jerusalem in January 1956. In the months following this visit Hammarskjöld was able to iron out a tentative peace settlement for the region.

4

The Suez Crisis

Deeper trouble was brewing in the Middle East. On July 26, 1956, the storm broke. President Nasser of Egypt, in an act designed to demonstrate Egypt's power, seized control of the Suez Canal.

The canal, though it lay in Egyptian territory, was considered an international waterway. One hundred and three miles long, it connects the Mediterranean Sea with the Red Sea, shortening a trip from the Atlantic Ocean to the Persian Gulf by 5,000 miles or more. It is a critical link in worldwide shipping, especially in carrying precious Middle Eastern oil to Western Europe and the United States. A French company had constructed the canal nearly 100 years earlier; Great Britain had bought a sizable interest in the canal in 1875. Both countries made huge profits from its ownership and operation. Hammarskjöld read with increasing concern reports of Nasser's nationalization of the canal. The story began on the night of July 26, in the city of Alexandria, Egypt, which was tense with excitement. Searchlights pierced the darkness and flags flapped in the breeze. Thousands of Egyptians, celebrating the fourth anniversary of the revolution that brought Nasser to power, assembled for an emotional speech from their leader.

At the induction to my present office I quoted these lines by a Swedish poet: 'The greatest prayer of man is not for victory, but for peace.'
—DAG HAMMARSKJÖLD

Hammarskjöld listens to a debate in the General Assembly in the mid-1950s. Two of the major UN concerns during this period were the 1956 Soviet invasion of Hungary and the continuing Arab-Israeli conflict, the solution to which seemed to slip repeatedly from Hammarskjöld's grasp.

On August 5, 1956, President Nasser delivered a rousing speech to his fellow Egyptians in Alexandria, declaring that Egypt would fight to maintain control over the Suez Canal. Nasser had nationalized the vital waterway on July 26.

Like "a demonic sorcerer conjuring up from the bowels of the earth the legions of hate and fury," Nasser spoke to his people for two hours. Working the crowd to a fever pitch, he attacked Israel, Britain, and other Western countries. Britain "sucked our blood and stole our rights." To the United States, which had just refused Egypt a loan, Nasser exclaimed, "Americans, may you choke in your fury!" Nasser finally concluded with the announcement that Egyptian soldiers were at that very moment seizing control of the Suez Canal. Revenues from the operation of the canal would finance the construction of a great dam on the Nile River. Wealth and power were finally within Egypt's grasp. The crowd went wild with delight.

Britain and France were outraged by Nasser's seizure of the canal and threatened to go to war with Egypt. For two months, in New York, Hammarskjöld worked steadily, trying to bring the concerned parties together to discuss the issue and to prevent the outbreak of war. Finally, on October 5, Hammarskjöld met with the foreign ministers of Egypt, Britain, and France; representatives from several other countries, including the United States and the Soviet Union, also attended. The secretary-general hammered out two resolutions that all three agreed on, but in the Security Council the Soviet Union vetoed the second resolution. Nonetheless, the first resolution went a long way toward resolving the problem, and by mid-October several points were adopted, the most important of which were open international passage through the Suez Canal and protection of the canal from political interference by any country.

Everyone was optimistic. The French foreign minister, Christian Pineau, declared, "We have been able to achieve results which, while incomplete, are nevertheless positive." Britain's foreign secretary, Selwyn Lloyd, left the UN to return to England, confident that negotiations between Britain and Egypt based on the UN resolution would soon begin.

In Britain, Prime Minister Anthony Eden had other ideas. He was worried about public opinion. The British public was growing impatient with the way he ran the government, and he was widely denounced as a weak leader. Wanting to change his image, he found the Suez crisis an opportunity for dramatic and forceful action. He met with the French leaders in Paris, and they agreed to meet force with force. They persuaded Israel, which felt threatened by Egyptian control of Suez, to join in as well.

On October 29, the first phase of the Israeli attack began. Sixteen transport planes took off from Israel and dropped 395 paratroopers at a strategic mountain pass in Egypt near the Suez Canal. To protect them, the British and French air forces bombed Egyptian airfields. French supply planes parachuted weapons and food to the Israeli troops. Israel soon sent a heavily armored column into Egypt to reinforce its paratroopers.

The attacks on Egypt caught the world by surprise. When the news reached New York, Hammarskjöld called an emergency session of the UN. The U.S. ambassador to the UN, Henry Cabot Lodge, was found by an assistant attending the opera, and he hurried off in white tie and tails to the UN. Together, he and Hammarskjöld drafted a cease-fire resolution for the Security Council, but after a long debate France and Britain voted against it.

The Security Council was unable to act in the face of the vetoes by France and Britain. Hammarskjöld

British Prime Minister Anthony Eden. Britain and France had cooperatively owned and operated the Suez Canal since the mid-1800s and were outraged by its nationalization. Trying to boost his sagging popularity at home, Eden threatened Egypt with attack if it did not relinquish control of the canal.

did not sleep that night, and in the morning his Swedish housekeeper, Nellie, found him still at work. He felt betrayed by France and Britain, which had made war on a single, small nation at a time when a peaceful settlement of the dispute was almost at hand.

A few hours later, the secretary-general stood by his chair at the center of the large horseshoe-shaped table of the Security Council. In a strained voice he lectured the council on the charter of the UN. Military aggression was a clear violation of UN principles. "A secretary-general cannot serve," he told them, unless "all member nations honor their pledges to observe all articles of the charter." The council members, including the British and French, all expressed their confidence in Hammarskjöld, but the vote was not changed. The secretary-general had to find another strategy to break the deadlock.

On October 29, 1956, the combined might of Israel, Britain, and France fell upon Egyptian troops occupying the Suez Canal region. Hammarskjöld and the UN, in an emergency session, drafted an overnight cease-fire, but Britain and France refused to sign it.

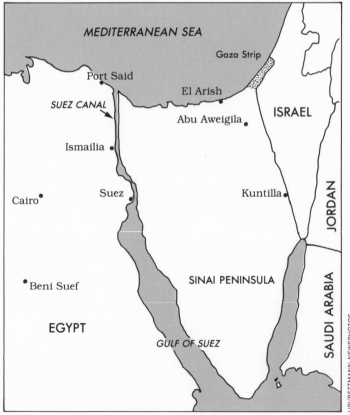

MEDITERRANEAN SEA

Gaza Strip

Port Said

El Arish

SUEZ CANAL

ISRAEL

Abu Aweigila

Ismailia

Cairo

Suez

Kuntilla

JORDAN

Beni Suef

SINAI PENINSULA

SAUDI ARABIA

EGYPT

GULF OF SUEZ

Hammarskjöld took the issue to the General Assembly, where a simple majority vote was needed for action. U.S. Secretary of State John Foster Dulles flew to New York to address the assembly. Arriving at the General Assembly during the debate, Dulles went to the speaker's platform and appealed for an immediate cease-fire in the Middle East. The delegates argued over the details of the proposal all night. The necessary resolution was finally passed, and the assembly adjourned at 4:20 A.M.

Ironically, the war was beginning to wind down of its own accord. Egypt's Nasser soon knew he was beaten. He could not fight the Israelis when they were joined by two major powers. France and Britain, he learned, were organizing an invasion force. He decided that if Egypt could not have the Suez Canal, then he would turn it into a useless trickle of muddy water.

He seized 47 ships belonging to the British-French Canal Company and filled them with concrete, sinking them in the shallow canal. The tops of these sunken ships poked above the surface of the water, making navigation impossible for any ship larger than a rowboat.

Hammarskjöld and the UN delegates, meanwhile, began discussions on creating some kind of UN Mid-

Israeli tanks speed toward the Suez Canal to hold the territory taken by the initial assault. While Britain and France led a combined land and sea attack from the Mediterranean, Israeli forces penetrated to the eastern banks of the canal.

dle East peacekeeping military force. France and Britain suggested that their own troops, already on their way to invade Egypt, might act in the name of the UN. No other troops, they assured the secretary-general, would be needed. To Hammarskjöld, this was like having a chicken thief guard the chickens. He turned down their offer.

Rebuffed, France and Britain insisted that their attack would continue until an effective UN force was in place in Egypt. Hammarskjöld was determined to have the UN work all weekend if necessary in order to get some kind of international military force on its way to the Middle East.

After working all night on a cease-fire resolution, the General Assembly met again the following night to discuss a UN peacekeeping force. By dawn they had passed a resolution asking Hammarskjöld to form a UN force within 48 hours. Hammarskjöld turned to one of his closest assistants to work out the details. The assistant was Ralph Bunche, an American diplomat of great skill who had won the Nobel Peace Prize for negotiating the Arab-Israeli armistice of 1949.

Hammarskjöld and Bunche went straight to work on organizing the force. By afternoon they had the basic blueprint ready. The plan established the first real international peace force in history, made up entirely of troops from small nations. It scuttled for good the French and British efforts to have their own armies put under the UN flag.

Many governments were reluctant to provide troops for the UN Emergency Force (UNEF) until

An Egyptian youth stares in disbelief at ruined streets and buildings in Port Said as a British tank stands sentinel. By the early hours of October 30, 1956, invading British and French forces had taken control of this Mediterranean port city.

they knew exactly the force's functions, places and duration of duty, and other matters. Hammarskjöld and Bunche worked on clarifying these issues.

One of the first countries Hammarskjöld requested troops from was Norway. The government there called an emergency meeting the same day but discovered there was a law against sending troops abroad. Emergency legislation was pushed through. The next morning Norway notified Hammarskjöld that troops were ready to leave for the Middle East that night.

At this point Hammarskjöld's attention was drawn to another matter. On November 4, the same day that the General Assembly gave him 48 hours to organize a UN military force for the Middle East, the Security Council asked him to "investigate and report" on the increasingly tense situation in Hungary. In that Soviet-bloc country in Eastern Europe mass demonstrations against the government had culminated, on October 30, in the formation of a new government, headed by Imre Nagy. Nagy promised free elections and requested that the Soviet troops withdraw from the country. He appealed to the UN for mediation and assistance.

The United Nations Security Council convenes in October 1956 in an attempt to draw up acceptable terms for peace in the Middle East.

51

On November 2 the Soviet Union invaded Hungary to destroy Nagy and his followers. The Soviet army encircled the capital city of Budapest as the Hungarian people took to the streets in a desperate fight against the enemy. Two days later, a few hours after Hammarskjöld was asked to investigate the situation, the world listened to the last agonized cries of Radio Budapest: "Help Hungary! Help us!" Nagy was soon arrested, and a new pro-Soviet government under János Kádár was installed. The Hungarian government refused to allow the UN to investigate and rejected Hammarskjöld's offer to go to Hungary.

Stymied by the refusal of Kádár's government to allow any investigation, by the opposition from the Soviet Union to any interference in Hungary or negotiation on the issue, and by the lack of support for the Hungarians from the Western nations, which feared a military confrontation with the Soviets, Hammarskjöld's hands were tied. As the free radio stations still operating in Hungary cried "What is the United Nations doing?" Hammarskjöld only managed to squeeze out of the General Assembly a resolution condemning the Soviet Union for its intervention in Hungary.

The 1956 Hungarian revolution was brutally suppressed, and a frustrated Hammarskjöld could only watch it happen. The UN and its secretary-general were severely criticized for not taking some kind of action in Hungary to rescue it from the clutches of the Soviet Union. During the crisis, thousands of Hungarians escaped from their country. Many went to the United States. Hammarskjöld knew that no government in the world went to the aid of Hungary during the crisis, yet many blamed the UN for not acting.

Nearly a year after the crisis had ended, the UN issued a report on Hungary. Based on testimony from refugees, it condemned the Soviet Union for depriving Hungary of its liberty and independence and for deporting thousands of people to Soviet labor camps.

The Middle East crisis had not subsided. The invasion of Egypt by France and Britain shocked the world. The Soviet Union reacted violently. The So-

The Russian vessel *Poti* (bottom) attempts to sail through the Suez Canal, strewn with the wreckage of nearly 50 ships ordered sunk by Nasser following the attack on Egypt by Israel, Britain, and France. Nasser's actions effectively blocked the canal.

viets and their allies in Europe had been supporting Nasser for some time and supplying him with military hardware. The Soviets threatened to use force if necessary "to crush the aggressors and restore peace in the Middle East." They warned that their rockets could reach France and other Western European countries and rain destruction upon them.

The Soviet threat sent the French government scurrying to call an emergency meeting in the middle of the night. Several cabinet members showed up in pajamas and robes. Yet France insisted that a UN force had to be in place at the canal before they would call off their attack. Egypt and Israel, in the meantime, had sent word to Hammarskjöld agreeing to the UN call for a cease-fire.

With the details of Hammarskjöld's plan for a UN peacekeeping force completed the following day, and pledges from several small countries to send troops, France and Britain finally agreed to a cease-

An enormous statue of former Soviet leader Joseph Stalin, covered with graffiti, is dragged from its pedestal in the Hungarian capital of Budapest, where a revolution toppled the pro-Soviet Hungarian government in October 1956. The new premier requested Hammarskjöld's help against Soviet invasion.

fire. By that time they had achieved their goal — control of the Suez Canal.

Within a few days of the cease-fire in Egypt, President Nasser allowed the first troops of the UNEF to enter his country. Forty-five blue-helmeted officers and men from Denmark and Norway made up the first contingent. The following day Hammarskjöld arrived with 54 troops from the South American nation of Colombia. Within four weeks the force numbered 3,700 men from eight nations. In another eight weeks it reached its full strength of 6,000 men from 10 countries. They took over from the British, French, and Israeli troops, which withdrew from the area.

The emergency force was a new concept in world history. It was a military force intended to prevent, not wage, war. As a genuine international arm of the UN, it was a great improvement over the UN effort in the Korean War a few years earlier. At that time the entire operation had been run by the United States.

The main duties of the UNEF at first were to clear

mines, patrol the area, and make sure that no other troops were active near the canal. Hammarskjöld sent Ralph Bunche, along with a general from Finland and one from Canada, to Egypt to administer this UN operation.

Hammarskjöld next tackled the problem of clearing the Suez Canal of the 47 ships which the Egyptians had sunk there. Britain and France sent a salvage fleet to the canal in an effort to regain some control of the situation, but Hammarskjöld wanted to exclude them from all UN operations in the area as long as there were any alternatives. He was determined that the Suez peacekeeping mission be a UN effort all the way. The head of the British navy scoffed at the idea of anyone else doing a competent job of clearing the canal, calling it "nonsense." Britain had the best salvage fleet in the world and no one, he insisted, could do the job better or faster.

To head the salvage job, Hammarskjöld recruited a top-level U.S. Army engineer, General Raymond ("Jack") Wheeler. Hammarskjöld borrowed 32 salvage ships from Belgium, Denmark, Sweden, West Germany, Italy, the Netherlands, and Yugoslavia. The salvage crew enjoyed trying to see if it could complete the job in less time than the British would have taken. It became a sport, and the crew cele-

> *For Hammarskjöld, the Suez exercise was enormously gratifying, not only because it meant another dangerous world crisis surmounted but equally because it testified to the indispensability of the UN.*
> —JOSEPH P. LASH
> writer and historian

Hammarskjöld (left) talks with UN Undersecretary Ralph Bunche of the United States, who oversaw UN mediation in the Suez Canal area. Bunche had won the Nobel Peace Prize in 1950 for his peacekeeping efforts in the Middle East.

brated every time they raised a ship. When they finished the job a few months later, General Wheeler announced that they had set new records in salvage work.

The British had estimated that their own navy could clear the canal in six months for a cost of $40 million. Wheeler did it in less than four months for only $8.2 million. On March 25, 1957, Hammarskjöld was there to watch the last ship raised from the canal.

Hammarskjöld now turned to the final problem: Israel's refusal to withdraw its troops completely from Egyptian territory. The Israelis were reluctant to evacuate certain areas along the border, especially the Gaza Strip, where Egyptian terrorist raids had habitually occurred over the years. Hammarskjöld spent several weeks talking with David Ben-Gurion and other Israeli leaders about this problem. When the United States and France offered Ben-Gurion assurances of future support, the reluctant Israelis finally agreed to withdraw their troops. With this the UN General Assembly concluded its longest session, and one of its most difficult ones.

A Dutch salvage ship pulls the massive hulk of the *Edgar Bonnet* from the bottom of the Suez Canal. The raising of this last wreck ended the four-month-long operation to clear the canal by a UN cooperative team from seven European nations.

During the Suez crisis, the UN was in a turmoil 24 hours a day for several days. There were constant meetings, interviews, reports, press conferences, and political maneuvering. Hammarskjöld dominated and controlled these events. His best qualities came out during crises such as this. His wide knowledge, his foresight, his powerful intellect, his skill in dealing with people, and his stamina, which kept him going for days at a time with hardly any sleep, made him the natural leader to whom others looked for guidance and direction.

A UN Emergency Force patrol marches through the vast desert of the Sinai Peninsula. In order to pacify the Egyptians as well as the Israelis, British, and French, the UN dispatched peacekeeping troops from several countries to the Suez region.

57

5

"Preventive Diplomacy"

Shortly before Hammarskjöld's five-year term as secretary-general was about to expire in 1957, the General Assembly took a vote on reelecting him. He won in a landslide. Not a single vote was cast against him. Eastern and Western nations, rich and poor nations, large and small nations, industrialized and underdeveloped nations — all voted for the man who had made the UN a respected and powerful force in the world.

Yet Hammarskjöld knew that his recent triumphs in keeping peace in the Middle East, for which he owed much of his reelection support, were fragile at best. In fact, another crisis there soon demanded his attention.

In early 1958 Egypt and Syria formed the United Arab Republic (UAR), an arrangement to work together on common problems. It represented an initial step in Egyptian President Nasser's attempt to unite all the Arabs in the Middle East under his own leadership. But other Arab countries did not trust him. Two weeks later, to offset Nasser's act, Jordan and Iraq joined in the Arab Union, which was promptly denounced by Nasser. The Egyptian leader's Arab nationalist appeal remained strong, however, and both Israel and many Western nations

> *The pursuit of peace and progress cannot end in a few years in either victory or defeat. The pursuit of peace and progress, with its trials and its errors, its successes and its setbacks, can never be relaxed and never abandoned.*
> —DAG HAMMARSKJÖLD

Hammarskjöld arrives at a London airport, 1956. After his tireless efforts to solve the Suez crisis, Hammarskjöld was unanimously reelected as UN secretary-general in 1957. Having proved his policy of personal diplomacy a success, the secretary-general continued to travel from one country to another around the world.

Rioters flee police in Beirut, Lebanon, in May 1957. Unrest accompanying attempts, backed by Arab nationalists in Egypt and Syria, to topple the pro-Western government of Lebanon's President Camille Chamoun eventually erupted into civil war.

were apprehensive about his effect on the weaker Arab countries.

Their concerns seemed justified in the case of Lebanon. This small nation to the north of Israel was torn by religious differences and had the additional weakness of an unpopular government. President Camille Chamoun's pro-Western policies had alienated the Lebanese Muslims, who, with the recent immigration of Palestinian refugees, now were in the majority. If the Lebanese government toppled it might be succeeded by a pro-Nasser government that would then join the UAR. Nasser began a daily radio campaign calling for Arab unity and raining insults on the Lebanese government. He also attacked Israel and the Western nations in these broadcasts.

Antigovernment riots soon broke out in Lebanon. The violence quickly led to a full-scale civil war, and the government appealed to the UN for help.

After arguing over whether the matter was truly international or merely an internal Lebanese problem, the UN delegates voted to send a team, named the UN Observation Group in Lebanon (UNOGIL).

60

Hammarskjöld said UNOGIL was not a military force like the UNEF but instead represented an attempt to prevent the conflict from spreading outside Lebanon and involving the major powers — and their cold war politics — in the Middle East. He called it "preventive diplomacy."

Two days after the passage of the UNOGIL resolution in June 1958, the first UN observers were on duty in Lebanon. It was important that the UNOGIL stay above any involvement in the Christian-Muslim conflict, but in order to get accurate reports, UNOGIL had to talk to both sides. Because of the delicate nature of the situation Hammarskjöld decided to go to Lebanon himself. It was a dangerous mission. Arriving in the capital city of Beirut, he found it the scene of heavy fighting. To protect him, the government provided him with an escort of four cars. One of his first trips with his armored escort was a visit to the Lebanese president, Chamoun, whom he found barricaded in his house, surrounded by tanks and barbed wire to protect him from rebel attack.

Hammarskjöld wasted no time while on this trip. His first day there began at five in the morning, and he worked straight through until the next morning. His meeting that day with the UN observers went long past dinner time. When one of the men complained that he was hungry, another one brought

Hammarskjöld passes a saluting guard on his way to meet with President Chamoun in his barricaded home in Beirut. The secretary-general made this risky trip to Lebanon in June 1958 to examine the situation firsthand and participate directly in the peace negotiations.

61

out a box of mangoes (an exotic fruit) and a bottle of whisky. This produced an unusual dinner, and Hammarskjöld later enjoyed telling others the story. When Hammarskjöld finally ended the meeting, at 2:30 in the morning, he asked for a book to read. He had finished reading it five and a half hours later when the meeting was resumed.

It was urgent that Hammarskjöld's mission to the Middle East succeed in ending the civil war in Lebanon. If it failed, the United States and Britain intended to send troops in to restore peace. If that happened, it was almost certain that the forces opposing the Lebanese government would blow up oil pipelines there as a way of getting back at the Americans and British.

Hammarskjöld next went to Cairo, Egypt. After long discussions, President Nasser promised Hammarskjöld that he would stop the transport of all weapons and ammunition into Lebanon from Syria and Egypt. Hammarskjöld accepted the offer, stating that Nasser "has never gone back on anything he said to me personally." To this, Nasser replied, "I wish to maintain that record."

Back in Beirut two days later, at a luncheon for Hammarskjöld, a huge cake was served for dessert. On the cake were inscribed the words, "UN, save Lebanon."

Hammarskjöld returned to New York confident that his talks with the various government leaders had gone well. He was optimistic that Egypt and Syria would soon stop their efforts to overthrow the Lebanese government, and that once outside interference ended, the Lebanese would find their own solutions.

Hammarskjöld's carefully negotiated plan worked well — for a time. Nasser kept his promise that he would stop sending troops and arms to the rebels in Lebanon, and he cut back the radio broadcasts attacking the Lebanese government. The UN observers in Lebanon duly reported these developments to the UN. Then the roof fell in.

On July 13, the army of Iraq, joined by an angry mob, swept into the Iraqi royal palace in Baghdad and murdered the king, the crown prince, and the

Soldiers of Iraq's new military government guard the charred remains of the royal palace in Baghdad. Following the assassination of Iraq's pro-Western king, crown prince, and prime minister in July 1958, a pro-Soviet regime took control.

UPI/BETTMANN NEWSPHOTOS

prime minister, who had all been supporters of the United States. With the government now in the hands of what appeared to be pro-Soviet forces, the United States felt it had to act to protect its remaining interests in the area. U.S. President Dwight D. Eisenhower feared that the revolution might spread to Lebanon.

The U.S. ambassador to the UN, Henry Cabot Lodge, consulted with Hammarskjöld. The secretary-general told him that U.S. intervention in Lebanon would destroy the UN effort to maintain the fragile peace. Lodge was distressed but believed that if the United States did not act immediately, it might be too late. The following day, U.S. Marines landed in Lebanon to bolster the shaky government there.

Nasser was outraged at this intervention by the United States. He went straight to Moscow to confer with the Soviet leaders. The Soviets, who up to now had been friends of Nasser, were unwilling to offer him any assistance. The unpredictable Soviet leader, Nikita Khrushchev, was afraid to act. The Americans had gone crazy, Khrushchev told Nasser. "We are not ready for World War III," he declared. Khrushchev advised Nasser to try to ride out the storm.

U.S. Marines land outside Beirut on July 15, 1958. Fearing that the recent revolution in Iraq would spread to Lebanon, U.S. President Dwight D. Eisenhower ordered American forces in to support Chamoun's weak government.

During a meeting of the UN Security Council on July 18, 1958, Hammarskjöld (center right) listens to U.S. delegate Henry Cabot Lodge. Hammarskjöld was outraged by the U.S. invasion of Lebanon, believing it threatened the imminent UN peace settlement there.

The Soviets and Egyptians were not the only leaders irritated by the American intervention. To Hammarskjöld as well it made little sense. The UN was on the verge of a political settlement in Lebanon, a peaceful solution to the civil war. The U.S. invasion threw that delicate situation into confusion. Moreover, Lebanon and Iraq had no common border. Lebanon was therefore not meant to provide a base for American action against Iraq. Such action could be conducted from the U.S. Mediterranean fleet and other Mediterranean bases already in existence.

Hammarskjöld was puzzled by the U.S. action and angry with President Eisenhower and Secretary of State Dulles. When Lodge made a report to the UN Security Council it became clear to Hammarskjöld that the American action was based on inaccurate information regarding the Iraqi revolt. As Hammarskjöld and others knew, it was not in fact anti-American.

The U.S. troop landing was almost a disaster. When the Marines arrived in Beirut, the capital of Lebanon, they seized control of the airport. Units of the Lebanese army, mistakenly ordered to resist the takeover, marched through the capital toward the airport. A confrontation was averted at the last minute by the U.S. ambassador, Robert McClintock. Seeing what was happening, he hurried out into the street to confer with the Lebanese army leader. They met between the advance guards of the two armies in order to avert a fight. Meanwhile Hammarskjöld instructed the UN observers to remain in Lebanon until the situation was clarified.

To combat the growing criticism of the invasion, the American government released a statement that its troops would cooperate and work with the UN observer group. Hammarskjöld realized that this would compromise the impartiality of the UN. He declared that there could be no "contact or working relationship, formal or informal, between UNOGIL and any non-Lebanese forces in Lebanon."

In the Security Council the Soviet Union demanded the immediate withdrawal from Lebanon of the U.S. forces. While a debate raged in the UN over this issue, King Hussein of Jordan, whose cousin had been the murdered king of Iraq, requested British troops to help protect him and his kingdom from the Iraqi revolutionaries. Britain sent in 2,500 paratroopers the next day.

It soon became clear that the new Iraqi government posed no threat to Lebanon or Jordan. American and British leaders became embarrassed over their military presence in those two countries. Red-faced, they went to Hammarskjöld and asked him to help get their troops out. They did not want to admit they had made an error. Somehow the world would have to be persuaded that although the situation was as dangerous as ever, another means of protecting Lebanon and Jordan had been found. Hammarskjöld soon came up with an answer.

UNOGIL could be enlarged, Hammarskjöld suggested, which would allow the United States to claim that its Marines were no longer needed in Lebanon. To help the British get out of Jordan, the UN observer group at the 1949 Israeli armistice line could be beefed up (Jordan shares a long border with Israel), and some kind of UN presence established in Jordan itself.

> *It is not the Soviet Union or, indeed, any other big powers who need the United Nations for their protection; it is all the others. In a sense the organization is first of all their organization.*
> —DAG HAMMARSKJÖLD

The Security Council became deadlocked over these proposals, so Hammarskjöld exercised his characteristic imagination and ingenuity. Constructing "a tangled thicket" of phrases from the UN Charter and paragraphs from proposed resolutions, Hammarskjöld conferred upon himself the authority to reinforce UNOGIL as he saw fit. The UN delegates, dazzled by the confusing jungle of words and glad to relinquish responsibility for the problem, approved the resolution and turned the issue over to Hammarskjöld. "Leave it to Dag," was a solution increasingly adopted by the UN delegates while Hammarskjöld was secretary-general.

With Hammarskjöld's diplomatic efforts leading the way, a political settlement was quickly reached in Lebanon. President Chamoun agreed to a compromise, and a new president was elected who was acceptable to both sides in the civil war.

By the end of the year the American and British troops were gone from Lebanon and Jordan, and Hammarskjöld had concluded the UNOGIL operation. The secretary-general emerged from the Lebanese crisis, according to one commentator, with "more personal prestige and power than ever before."

Another opportunity for Hammarskjöld's preventive diplomacy arose in 1959 in Laos, a small country in Indochina, west of Vietnam. When France, the colonial ruler of Indochina, pulled out of the area in 1954, Laos was divided between a group of pro-communist leaders, called the Pathet Lao, in the north and a Western-oriented government in the south. In June 1959 the right-wing, pro-Western government of Premier Phoui Sananikone charged that communist troops from North Vietnam were crossing the border. The government requested the UN to send an emergency force to halt the attack.

Realizing that Laos was of strategic interest to both the United States and the Soviet Union, Hammarskjöld selected an observer group from nations not involved in cold war politics to monitor the situation. After spending a month in Laos, the group reported that it could find no "flagrant aggression" by North Vietnamese troops.

Laotian Premier Phoui Sananikone confers with Ham-
marskjöld in 1959. After the
premier complained to the
UN that his country was
being threatened by Soviet-
backed communist aggres-
sion from Vietnam, Hammarskjöld provided Laos with a
UN observer group and tech-
nological and economic aid.

Seizing the initiative, Hammarskjöld announced
his intention of establishing a UN representative in
Laos who could keep him informed of day-to-day
developments there. He went to the country himself
to prepare the way and to urge a policy of neutrality
on the Laotian government. He decided that economic and technical assistance was needed to help
the government and its people with some of their
problems, and he assigned a small technical staff to
proceed with that work.

Hammarskjöld's efforts in Laos kept the country
at peace only while he was secretary-general. The
Soviet Union believed that the UN presence there
inhibited the spread of the communist movement,
and the Soviet leaders repeatedly expressed their
opposition to the UN work in Laos. This episode
marked the beginning of the Soviet Union's increasing dissatisfaction with Hammarskjöld, a dissatisfaction that would grow to become one of the most
serious crises in the history of the UN.

6

"Humility, Loyalty, and Devotion to Duty"

Early in Hammarskjöld's career as secretary-general, most UN employees smiled at his appeals for "humility, loyalty, and devotion to duty" and his other noble statements. They were used to hearing world leaders and diplomats express similar virtuous thoughts without ever expecting anyone to take them too seriously. As one UN employee later wrote: "This was, after all, the way the perfect secretary-general ought to express himself. . . . It was not realized at all that the new secretary-general meant every word that he said." Hammarskjöld's integrity and high ideals were in fact important elements in his ability as an international leader to command respect and get things done.

Hammarskjöld liked to lead from the frontline and take personal responsibility for UN actions. He did not want to have any special efforts made to protect him from possible danger. A strong believer in personal contact, he traveled widely to meet the leaders of as many countries as possible. His extensive travel sometimes drew fire from one or another of the big powers. His response was always the same: "He [the secretary-general] has to find out for him-

Dag Hammarskjöld was the most remarkable man I have ever seen or worked with. . . . I learned more from him than from any other man.
—RALPH BUNCHE
UN official and Nobel Peace Prize winner

A popular figure in developing nations such as India, Hammarskjöld receives traditional welcoming gifts of flowers and food from villagers outside the capital of New Delhi. The secretary-general made it a policy to visit as many UN member nations as possible.

Issued in 1958, a United Nations stamp commemorates the UN Economic and Social Council. To Hammarskjöld, one of the most important missions of the UN was to improve the living conditions of small, third world nations.

Once [Hammarskjöld] rushed out of a meeting, gazed for a while at an abstract painting in his office and sighed, "Now I am refreshed." Then he returned to the meeting.
—EMERY KELEN
UN staff member

self, and that may mean . . . that he has to go himself."

As secretary-general, Hammarskjöld was almost constantly surrounded by television cameras and reporters. There were close to a hundred newspaper reporters assigned to the UN on a daily basis, and that number jumped to several hundred if something important was going on. Since Hammarskjöld, who was optimistic but realistic about his effectiveness, never made public statements intended to dramatize events, reporters were often irritated or puzzled by him. The French called him the "master of the calculated imprecision."

Hammarskjöld's vague language was simply a diplomatic way of saying things that could not be twisted or oversimplified. Also, he was constantly being pressed for statements about events and situations that were themselves complicated and unclear. Many diplomats and newspaper reporters complained about his "Swedish English." One member of a UN delegation pulled out a magnifying glass he claimed to use for reading Hammarskjöld's handwriting and then added that he had not yet found a similar device for his ears. But clever listeners could often figure out the hidden meanings behind the secretary-general's words. His remarks had great meaning if understood as an ongoing discussion with government leaders and diplomats around the world.

On the other hand, when not speaking about political crises or delicate diplomatic events, Hammarskjöld could be quite clear and straightforward. He was often asked to speak at public ceremonies, and his message was always the same: the need for the brotherhood of all people everywhere; for reason, cooperation, communication; and, above all, for peaceful solutions to all problems.

Hammarskjöld frequently impressed people with the breadth and depth of his interests and knowledge. When he decided to decorate the walls of the UN buildings with some works of art, he arranged to borrow a few pieces from New York's Museum of Modern Art. As he strolled through the galleries with members of the museum staff, he discussed modern

Hammarskjöld proudly
stands before French artist
Fernan Léger's "Woman
Combing Her Hair," lent by
the Museum of Modern Art in
New York City for display in
the UN buildings. His interest and considerable knowledge on a wide variety of subjects often astounded those
he met.

art so professionally that his hosts invited him to
make a speech on the subject at the museum's 25th
anniversary celebration later in the year.

Hammarskjöld was also intensely interested in
serious literature, and when his father died in late
1953, he was elected to take his father's place as a
member of the prestigious Swedish Royal Academy,
one of whose duties is to award the Nobel Prizes. It
was the first time a son had succeeded his father
as a member of the academy. At his inauguration
in 1954, Hammarskjöld stood before the Swedish
royal family, government leaders, and the other
members of the academy and gave a speech about
his father.

Hammarskjöld was extremely well-read in the
classics and modern literature and translated modern works from English, French, and German into
Swedish. He was constantly on the lookout for ways
to help writers. He once convinced a poorly schooled
but highly motivated man from Lapland, the wild
Arctic area of northern Sweden, to record his knowledge of his people before their ancient culture was

Exploring another of his scholarly interests, Hammarskjöld chats with renowned Jewish philosopher and author Martin Buber in January 1959 at the Hebrew University in Jerusalem.

swallowed up by the modern world. After writing a best-selling book on the subject, the man expressed his gratitude to Hammarskjöld, saying that "without the new frankness and assurance which Dag gave me, I would surely never have dared make it my aim to write down all the old tales and stories which the old ones had told me in my youth."

Hammarskjöld was admired not only for his work on behalf of others but for the amount of work he could accomplish himself. One reason for his extraordinary productivity was that he never wasted any time. He often left his companions breathing hard just trying to keep up with him while walking. He maintained such a pace even on vacation. His UN bodyguard once tried to slow him down by getting him to stop to take pictures as they hurried along a quiet beach in Sweden. Hammarskjöld was an avid photographer and often carried a camera, so his bodyguard, gasping and panting by his side, would point out promising subjects, and while Hammarskjöld paused for a moment his companions would stop and catch their breath.

Hammarskjöld loved the outdoors and spent as much time as he could spare hiking and camping. He grew to love New York, his second home, but he never lost the deep feelings he harbored for his native land. He bought a farmhouse in Backåkra, in southern Sweden, to which he retreated for peace and solitude.

Always interested in nature and art, Hammarskjöld took advantage of his wide traveling to work on his photography. An unusual photographic opportunity arose in the spring of 1960 when Hammarskjöld went to Nepal at the request of the government there to discuss a boundary dispute. The official business was not very important when compared to the other issues demanding his time, but this remote country boasted one of the most spectacularly beautiful places in the world — the Himalayas. Sprawling across the area between China and India, this mountain range is called "the top of the world" and contains Mount Everest, the highest mountain in the world, the summit of which was reached for the first time only a few weeks after Hammarskjöld had become secretary-general. In a tribute from one mountain climber to another, Tenzing Norgay, who along with Sir Edmund Hillary was the first person to reach the top of Everest, had presented to Hammarskjöld the ice ax he had carried on that famous climb. Hammarskjöld hung it in an honored place, above the fireplace in his New York apartment.

While in Nepal, Hammarskjöld accepted the king's offer of his personal airplane and pilot for a flight into the mountains where he could see them up close and take pictures. The small plane could not fly above 15,000 feet, well below the soaring mountain peaks, so as the pilot steered the plane through the valleys and narrow passes, Hammarskjöld, in the copilot's seat, took picture after picture of the greatest mountain range on earth.

Hammarskjöld also visited the most famous of the Buddhist shrines in Nepal, calling it the "dream of a world beyond pain and vicissitude in the shadow of the timeless mountain." After returning to New York he wrote an article about his trip. Along with some of his best pictures, it was published in the *National Geographic* magazine.

In March 1959 Hammarskjöld visited the Soviet Union at Nikita Khrushchev's invitation. Treated with the courtesy of a visiting chief of state, Ham-

Actor-comedian Danny Kaye (standing, left) and opera virtuoso Ezio Pinza (seated) frolic with the UN secretary-general during the UN Staff Day party on September 8, 1953. Hammarskjöld was well known for his charming manners and good nature.

He could enthuse insignificant persons to achieve results beyond their ability.
—GUNNAR MYRDAL
Swedish economist and sociologist, on Hammarskjöld

marskjöld attended receptions, met with collective farmers, and saw an industrial fair. Yet his hosts regarded his political beliefs with suspicion. At one reception, when Hammarskjöld offered a toast to "honest sinners now on record," Khrushchev and Deputy Premier Anastas Mikoyan thought he was referring to Soviet writers who were critical of the government and declined to raise their glasses with him. When he later offered another toast, this time to "living Soviet art," Khrushchev asked him what he meant by that. Hammarskjöld replied that each person could define it for himself, and only then did the Soviet leaders join him in the toast.

During this visit Hammarskjöld mentioned that as a member of the Swedish Academy he had voted for Soviet writer Boris Pasternak, the author of the novel *Dr. Zhivago*, for the Nobel Prize. The Soviet government had refused to allow publication of the book because of its critical treatment of the 1917 Russian Revolution, and Pasternak had been forbidden to go to Sweden to accept the prize. Mikoyan asked Hammarskjöld how he, as secretary-general, could associate himself with such political views. Hammarskjöld believed that literature was separate from politics, so he simply mentioned that one of

Pursuing one of his favorite passions, Hammarskjöld relaxes in the mountains of Sweden. Although he came to feel at home in New York, Hammarskjöld never lost his love for the stark beauty of his homeland.

Mikoyan's favorite writers, Fyodor Dostoevsky, had written his famous novel *Crime and Punishment* about the murder of an old lady — did Mikoyan therefore approve of the killing of old ladies? As Mikoyan reddened with embarrassment, Khrushchev roared with laughter.

Shortly before Hammarskjöld left the country, Khrushchev took him for a short trip in a rowboat on the Black Sea. There was no conversation while Khrushchev rowed his guest through the water because Russian was one language Hammarskjöld did not know and there was no room in the small boat for an interpreter. Hammarskjöld later wrote to thank Khrushchev for his hospitality and mentioned that "although the boat trip was a bit on the silent side, not because of a lack of will but because there was no place for an interpreter, I shall always remember it with great pleasure. I have carefully noted that next time you will leave it to me to row you." What he and Khrushchev did not know was that the next time they met it would be as bitter enemies.

Onlookers watch at a reception in Moscow as Soviet Premier Nikita Khrushchev converses with Hammarskjöld. Despite some tense moments, Hammarskjöld thought his March 1959 trip to the Soviet Union a success.

75

7

African Nightmare

When Hammarskjöld was first elected secretary-general in 1953, only four African nations were members of the UN. But the age of colonial empires was ending; the colonial peoples themselves had demanded its end. They wanted freedom and independence and the right to govern themselves, and the old imperialist countries — Great Britain, France, Belgium — reluctantly began to grant their colonies the independence they sought. One by one, they allowed them to begin electing their own representative governments, their own executive officers, their own judges. When the period of apprenticeship was over, a great ceremony, full of pomp and pageantry, heralded the birth of a new nation. During Hammarskjöld's eight years in office, 22 African nations achieved independence and joined the UN. The secretary-general was deeply concerned about the creation of these new states. These new nations, Hammarskjöld believed, must not become puppets of their former masters nor pawns in the Cold War between the United States and the Soviet Union.

By 1960 the situation in Africa had become crucial to Hammarskjöld's efforts to keep peace in the world. Early in that year he made a six-week tour of the continent to determine whether any of the fledgling republics needed UN assistance. Every-

> *It is for the African states themselves to define the elements which establish the basis for African solidarity. It is also for them to find and define the aims which this regional community should pursue.*
> —DAG HAMMARSKJÖLD

A distraught Hammarskjöld addresses a special night session of the UN Security Council in September 1960. The meeting was convened to discuss the explosive situation in the African nation of the Congo.

where he went, the red carpet was rolled out for the man who had made the UN a major force in world affairs.

Hammarskjöld was particularly concerned with the Belgian Congo, a large, central African country one-third the size of the United States. The Congolese people had only recently mounted a significant independence movement, and the Belgian government had decided to pull out before the people were adequately prepared for self-government. As the time approached for Congolese independence, the secretary-general assigned Ralph Bunche as a special UN representative to the country to report on developments there.

Hammarskjöld's concern proved to be justified. On June 30, 1960, Belgium granted independence to the newly named Republic of the Congo. But at the time there were no Congolese doctors or engineers, no experienced administrators, and no native officers in the army. Many Belgians remained to fill these positions of leadership.

Ominous events plagued the independence ceremonies. A Congolese man grabbed the Belgian king's ceremonial sword and ran off with it. Later, amid speeches of friendship and goodwill, the Congolese prime minister, Patrice Lumumba, com-

Belgium's Premier Gaston Eyskens (seated, right) and Congo's Prime Minister Patrice Lumumba meet in Léopoldville, the capital of the Congo, on June 30, 1960, to sign an act declaring independence for the Republic of the Congo.

plained bitterly of the hardships inflicted for many years on the Africans by the Belgians and other colonial powers.

A few days after the establishment of the new nation, members of the Congolese army turned against their Belgian officers and were soon attacking Belgian civilians as well. There were numerous incidents of harassment, beatings, and rapes. Bunche reported to Hammarskjöld on the rapid disintegration of order. Many Belgians were fleeing the country in panic, and when some civilians were killed by the mutineers, the Belgian government sent paratroopers in to protect those remaining. This military invasion angered Prime Minister Lumumba, and he appealed to the UN for military help to expel the Belgian troops and help restore order.

Hammarskjöld cut short a trip to Europe and rushed back to UN headquarters in New York to deal

Fearing for their lives, Belgian families flee Léopoldville. After Belgium had granted the Congo its independence many Belgians remained in the country to work as engineers, military personnel, and doctors. Many fell victim to the vengeful Congolese military.

with the emergency. He met immediately with the African UN delegations. After obtaining their approval and support he requested that the UN Security Council meet to discuss the situation. In an all-night session the Security Council debated the issue and the next morning passed a resolution giving Hammarskjöld the authority to act.

Within 48 hours the first UN troops were in the Congo. Within another 48 hours the UN force numbered 3,500, all from four African nations—Tunisia, Morocco, Ghana, and Ethiopia. Hammarskjöld was fully aware of the importance and difficulty of the undertaking. He reported to the Security Council that "the UN has embarked on its single biggest effort under UN colors, organized and directed by the UN itself"—an effort that would be decisive "not only for the future of the [UN] Organization but also for the future of Africa. And the future of Africa," he concluded, "may well in present circumstances mean the world."

The secretary-general had already met with an unexpected, serious complication. On July 11, Katanga, one of six large provinces making up the Republic of the Congo, declared its independence as a separate nation. Katangese secession was seen by many as a Belgian plot. The richest and most productive Congo province, developed with heavy investment from such Western countries as Belgium, France, and Great Britain, Katanga had announced its independence as soon as the Belgian paratroopers had landed.

The secession of Katanga posed a difficult problem for Hammarskjöld. Whose side should the UN take? And how should it proceed without alienating one side or the other? Hammarskjöld decided that the UN military force must replace the Belgian troops in Katanga just as they had done elsewhere in the Congo. But the UN would take no part in Congo politics, neither forcing Katanga to rejoin the Congo nor helping it to remain independent.

Yet Moise Tshombe, the president of Katanga, warned that he would "resist by every means" the entry of any UN troops into the state. Hammarskjöld was just as determined to send the troops in. To

A Léopoldville citizen is detained by Belgian paratroopers during an identification check. Soon after the anti-Belgian riots began in the Congo, Belgium sent troops into the nation to protect its citizens there.

meet this unexpected show of defiance, Hammarskjöld sought authority from the Security Council for UN troops to forcibly enter the province.

After ordering the UN command in the Congo to prepare to move into Katanga on 12 hours' notice, Hammarskjöld called the Security Council into session. He repeated his conviction that the UN must act in the best interests of the people of the Congo as a whole. This meant that it must first remove all foreign interference, safeguard democratic rights, and guarantee the freedom of all political views. He feared that a war in the Congo could lead to a wider war, possibly involving the great powers and nuclear weapons.

The secretary-general concluded his appeal to the Security Council by stating that the Europeans needed to respect the independence of the Congo to ensure a harmonious relationship with the Congolese people in the future. The Security Council worked all night before agreeing and voting on an acceptable resolution. The final agreement clearly defined the purpose of the UN involvement in the

UPI/BETTMANN NEWSPHOTOS

KATANGA ANAWATAKIA UJO WEMA

WELCOME TO FREE KATANGA
BIENVENUE AU KATANGA

"Welcome to Free Katanga," reads a sign outside the Elisabethville airport in the capital city of the newly declared independent nation of Katanga. Previously the wealthiest of the Congolese provinces, Katanga seceded on July 11, 1960.

Congo as the restoration of order, which would prepare for the withdrawal of the Belgian troops. The basic principles of the Congo operation were to be strictly enforced: the UN troops could use weapons only in self-defense, and they would remain independent of all Congolese internal politics.

Armed with new authority, Hammarskjöld decided to lead the UN operation himself. He arrived in the Congo on July 28, intending to explain the aims, as well as the limitations, of the UN operation to the Congolese leaders. In Léopoldville Hammarskjöld found Lumumba's government obsessed with the loss of Katanga, and he hastened to assure the Congolese ministers of UN impartiality. But the secretary-general was convinced that if the Belgian troops, whom the officials in Léopoldville believed were backing up the Katangese secession, were not removed soon, the UN mission would fail. Impressed by the urgency of the situation, Hammarskjöld decided to go to Katanga for talks with Tshombe. He took off for Elisabethville, the capital of Katanga, on the morning of August 12. His plane was followed by four planes carrying advisers and two companies of Swedish troops, which were to be stationed in Katanga.

At the Elisabethville airport, Tshombe was determined to keep the UN military force out of the province. Two hundred Katanga troops stood ready for action. A convoy of vehicles, including five trucks, a fire engine, and a bus, waited nearby, ready to be moved onto the runway to prevent the troop planes from landing. As the planes approached, the control tower radioed to Hammarskjöld that the four troop carriers would not be allowed to land.

Hammarskjöld argued by radio for 25 minutes

Map of the Congo in 1960, detailing the provinces and their capitals. Lumumba denounced the secession of Katanga as a Belgian plot to destroy the new republic, and the threat of civil war hung over the country.

while the planes circled the airfield. Finally, when he said that he would not land himself unless the other planes were also allowed to land, Tshombe surrendered, explaining that there had been a misunderstanding. It was enormously risky for the secretary-general to force his way into such a clearly threatening situation, yet, as he stepped out of his plane, he was greeted by a broadly smiling Tshombe, who handed him a tourist brochure entitled "Elisabethville Invites You."

Hammarskjöld refused Tshombe's offer to have him driven immediately away from the airport. He insisted on first seeing that the UN troops deplaned without any trouble. While that operation was being completed, a crowd shouted defiance at Hammarskjöld and the troops. Nonetheless, the Swedish troops took control of the airport, and only then did

Hammarskjöld (left, in white) convinces the Security Council to give him the power to send UN troops to replace the Belgian soldiers in Katanga. The Katangese, however, threatened to resist any UN interference in their country.

Hammarskjöld leave with Tshombe to discuss the UN role in Katanga. The following day a report was issued announcing the timetable for the removal of Belgian troops and the introduction of additional UN troops into Katanga. For the moment Hammarskjöld seemed to have defused the Katanga time bomb.

Hammarskjöld's success in Katanga was, as one writer put it, "daring and unprecedented." Faced with threats of armed resistance, the secretary-general, at great personal risk, had with leadership and courage brought the UN into the rebel province. Within four weeks all Belgian combat troops had left Katanga.

Hammarskjöld's triumph quickly led to new difficulties. Although the Belgian troops were leaving the province, Tshombe continued to maintain the province's independence. Lumumba was outraged that the UN force had not been placed at his own disposal to be used to force Katanga back under the rule of the Congo government in Léopoldville. The Soviet Union, looking to gain some influence in cen-

Katangese President Moise Tshombe greets the UN secretary-general in Elisabethville, Katanga. Hammarskjöld disregarded Tshombe's warnings and led a small force of UN troops into Katanga to force a meeting with the secessionist leader.

Swedish members of the UN forces secure the Elisabethville airport. Hammarskjöld's talks with Tshombe led to the removal of all Belgian troops from Katanga as well as an acceptance of another UN force to stabilize the region.

tral Africa, was equally upset, viewing Hammarskjöld's conduct as a screen behind which the Belgians would continue to control the wealth of Katanga.

Hammarskjöld left the Congo convinced that Lumumba's personal ambitions might destroy the Congo and the UN operation there. Lumumba's attitude had changed after Soviet leader Nikita Khrushchev promised him assistance; the Congolese prime minister, encouraged by the thought of Soviet support, seemed more interested in securing power for himself than in finding a peaceful solution to the Congo's problems. The Soviet Union was already the only nation contributing food to the Congo directly instead of through the UN. The Soviets were soon sending more than food: 17 transport planes complete with Russian crews — one for the personal use of Lumumba—and 100 trucks.

The UN Security Council endorsed Hammarskjöld's actions regarding Katanga and supported his impartial use of the UN force. Hammarskjöld asked the Soviet government about its direct assistance to the Congo, pointing out that it had earlier protested when the U.S. had sent 20 soldiers to help bring in UN supplies and troops. The Soviets replied that the Congo was still free to accept aid from any source.

Yet the Soviet action undermined one of the main purposes of the UN effort — to prevent direct intervention by the big powers. The Soviets vetoed a resolution introduced in the Security Council by Ceylon and Tunisia calling for member states to channel all aid through the UN, calling it an attempt to create a UN colony. Khrushchev accused Hammarskjöld of being a tool of "the colonialists and imperialists."

Hammarskjöld's impartiality got him into trouble with the Western nations as well, especially Belgium. Although Belgian combat troops had left Katanga after Hammarskjöld had brought UN troops in to replace them, Belgium continued to send civil and military advisers into the province. Hammarskjöld repeatedly protested against the Belgian government's delays and the misleading and false information it sent to the UN and to reporters.

The Congolese army, irregularly paid, poorly fed, divided by tribal differences, yet well-armed, was a bomb waiting to go off. The army's commander was reported afraid of his own troops. At times individual army units acted independently to harass UN personnel, European civilians, or rival tribes. Lumumba used the army to interfere with the UN civilians in an effort to force them to leave the country. There were incidents of beatings of "Belgian spies disguised as UN personnel."

The Congolese government was financially bankrupt as well, with no taxes and therefore no revenue.

Just as the secretary-general is the servant of the United Nations and not of any single nation, so he is obligated to risk himself in the interest of a just solution.
—DAG HAMMARSKJÖLD

It had to appeal to the UN for funds to pay and feed the army. Both the rival factions of the government were critical of the UN because of its policy of neutrality — each wanted the international organization on its own side as an ally. To add to the confusion, each faction sent its own representative to the UN. It was a unique situation for Hammarskjöld and the UN, one that could only lead to trouble. Hammarskjöld called the crisis in the Congo, a country "hustling headlong on the road to disintegration and chaos," a nightmare.

Following his successful coup in September 1960, Joseph Mobutu announces the military's accession to power. Demonstrating his pro-Western leanings, Mobutu holds a picture of Soviet Premier Khrushchev, with the words "Hands Off The Congo" in French.

While rival political groups fought with each other, the chief of staff of the Congolese army, Joseph Mobutu, marched his own troops into parliament and took over the slack reins of government himself. The hidden hand of Belgium, supported by the United States (which also had economic interests in the area), seemed to be behind the Mobutu takeover.

Mobutu soon expelled from the country the Soviet ambassador and all other pro-Soviet ambassadors. Khrushchev reacted violently. Blaming Hammarskjöld and the UN for the increasingly pro-Western developments in the Congo, Khrushchev launched a bitter attack on the secretary-general.

An emergency session of the General Assembly was called to take a vote on continuing Hammarskjöld's Congo policies. The members overwhelmingly endorsed the secretary-general, 70 to 0, with 11 abstentions. The UN vote was comforting to the secretary-general, but storm clouds loomed on the horizon.

Caught in the rivalry between East and West, between the interests of industrialized countries and the ambitions of underdeveloped nations, entirely dependent on the support of the UN member nations to carry out his policies, Hammarskjöld was again reminded that his was "the most impossible job on this earth." He would soon be confronted by dramatic new changes in the Congo. Of more immediate concern was the fact that Khrushchev was coming to New York to confront Hammarskjöld and the UN delegates in person.

I am hopeful — that's a professional weakness; hopeful and insistent.
—DAG HAMMARSKJÖLD
on his way to the Congo

8

Khrushchev Pounds the Desk

As the imperialist nations withdrew their colonial administrations from the Third World (as the underdeveloped and developing countries of the world came to be called), Khrushchev hoped to gain new allies there in the ongoing Cold War between the communist and the Western nations. The UN was becoming a "third force" in helping the new nations achieve independence, and Hammarskjöld was determined to keep the big powers from interfering in this process. Khrushchev was just as determined to bring the newly independent nations under the Soviet sphere of influence.

Twenty-three heads of government and 57 foreign ministers (or secretaries of state) met on the East Side of New York to open the 15th session of the UN General Assembly in September 1960. It would prove to be a memorable UN session. The growing UN presence around the world and its role in the Congo had made the young organization the center of international debate. Thirteen new African states, including the Republic of the Congo, were being admitted to membership in the UN at this

> *Mr. Hammarskjöld has always been biased with regard to the socialist countries, he has always upheld the interests of the U.S. and other countries of monopoly capital.*
> —NIKITA S. KHRUSHCHEV
> Soviet leader

Hammarskjöld on the rostrum during a UN General Assembly meeting. The secretary-general successfully guided the United Nations through numerous crises only to face continually fierce opposition in the UN halls.

United Nations headquarters, New York City. The two main buildings, the Secretariat and the General Assembly, stand behind the conference area. At the 15th session of the General Assembly, in September 1960, Hammarskjöld faced the greatest challenges to his power.

FIFTEENTH ANNIVERSARY **4**c

WE THE PEOPLES OF THE UNITED NATIONS

DETERMINED TO SAVE SUCCEEDING GENERATIONS FROM THE SCOURGE OF WAR...

1945 24 OCTOBER 1960

QUINZIEME ANNIVERSAIRE 十五週年紀念

A 1960 postage stamp commemorating the 15th anniversary of the founding of the United Nations. Details include the opening words to the preamble of the UN charter and border type reading "Fifteenth Anniversary" in English, French, Spanish, Chinese, and Russian.

session. Their representatives at the UN would be part of the very interested audience that would now judge the performances of Khrushchev, Hammarskjöld, and the other prominent world leaders. These representatives would have to tell their governments which side they should support.

Khrushchev proved to be an outlandish attention-getter. He tried to upset the routine of the General Assembly with wild behavior — heckling the speakers and calling them names, pounding his fists and one of his shoes on his desk. Outside the UN, Khrushchev gave spur-of-the-moment news conferences, sometimes causing traffic jams, and led a group of people on the sidewalk in singing "The Star-Spangled Banner."

The colorful Soviet leader had an emotional meeting with Fidel Castro, the new leader of Cuba. They met at the UN, hugged each other like old friends, and exchanged words neither could understand: one spoke Russian, the other Spanish. Castro and his companions had stormed out of their New York hotel after the management had complained about their cooking food in the rooms. At the UN, Castro made a four-and-a-half-hour speech denouncing the United States but did not criticize the secretary-general or the UN operation in the Congo.

U.S. President Dwight Eisenhower opened the session on September 20, speaking to the assembly in support of Hammarskjöld and the work of the UN in the Congo and elsewhere. Khrushchev addressed the assembly later the same day, and for two hours he attacked the U.S. and the other Western nations.

Then the Soviet leader turned on Hammarskjöld, accusing him of siding with the Belgians and other colonialists in the UN Congo operation. He proposed that the office of the secretary-general be abolished and replaced by a three-member executive. Each member would represent one of the three major political alignments in the world — the communists (or Eastern bloc), the capitalists (or Western bloc), and the neutral, or nonaligned, nations, led by such countries as India, Egypt, and Yugoslavia. Such an arrangement, everyone knew, would greatly weaken the executive and prevent the kind of forceful action

Accompanied by a considerable police escort, Prime Minister Fidel Castro of Cuba (center) and Nasser of Egypt (waving, center left) tour New York's Harlem section in September 1960. Their presence contributed to a stormy and memorable UN session.

Credit sidebar (vertical): UPI/BETTMANN NEWSPHOTOS

An angry crowd of demonstrators protests the presence of communist leaders at the 15th session of the UN General Assembly. The participation of Soviet leader Khrushchev was especially denounced.

Everyone has heard now how vigorously the imperialist countries defend Mr. Hammarskjöld's position. Is it not clear, then, in whose interest he interprets and executes . . . whose 'saint' he is?

—NIKITA S. KHRUSHCHEV
Soviet leader, to the UN
General Assembly

for which Hammarskjöld was famous. It would end the UN's effectiveness as a protector of weak nations and as an arbiter in major diplomatic disputes. As Khrushchev finished his speech he looked over at Hammarskjöld and smiled. The secretary-general, containing his anger, looked straight ahead.

There were now some anxious moments. If the nonaligned African nations joined with the pro-Soviet African nations to support Khrushchev's proposal, Hammarskjöld could be in real trouble. But the support Khrushchev had counted on did not materialize. One after another the Africans rose and stated their support for Hammarskjöld's policies. One of the most sympathetic to the Soviet viewpoint even scolded Khrushchev for bad manners.

When Hammarskjöld finally took the floor to reply, his voice was drained of emotion, and he spoke in a flat tone, as though he were reading a routine document. He emphasized that it was a question of the institution, not the man. The institution had to be impartial and objective, even if it sometimes tended to block the political aims of certain countries. The small nations of the world were entirely dependent on this impartial attitude and conduct to protect them from "the worldwide fight for power and influence." If the office of secretary-general was going to be destroyed, Hammarskjöld went on, he would rather see it "break on strict adherence to the principles of independence, impartiality and objectivity than drift on the basis of compromise." At these words an ovation rose through the assembly, and as it grew louder, Khrushchev joined in by pounding his fists on his desk. Hammarskjöld won this round, but Khrushchev would soon try again.

A few days later, Khrushchev further upset the proceedings. Shouting from his desk, he interrupted several speakers, including Prime Minister Harold Macmillan of Britain. He interrupted a speech by the Philippine delegate, calling him a stooge and a lackey of the United States. During the same speech, he took off his shoe, waved it in the air, and banged his desk with it. The president of the assembly, Frederick Boland of Ireland, trying to maintain order, pounded the gavel so hard and so often it finally broke under the strain.

Two days later, when Khrushchev went to the podium to speak, he resumed his attack on the secretary-general. Accusing Hammarskjöld of always defending the interests of the United States and other capitalist countries, he challenged him to quit his post. "If he himself does not muster up enough courage to resign, so to say, in a chivalrous man-

U.S. President Dwight D. Eisenhower opens the 1960 session of the General Assembly with praise for the UN and Hammarskjöld. Eisenhower voiced his support for UN policy in the Congo, knowing Khrushchev would attack the secretary-general on that subject.

At the 1960 General Assembly meeting, a flamboyant Khrushchev points an accusing finger as he rails against Hammarskjöld's policies. Khrushchev proposed that the position of secretary-general be replaced by a three-member executive board, thus weakening the UN command structure.

95

Hammarskjöld, in an emotional speech that brought him a standing ovation, refused to bow to Soviet pressure to resign. The secretary-general here says good-bye to Khrushchev before the Soviet leader returns home.

ner," Khrushchev concluded, "then we shall draw the necessary conclusions."

When Hammarskjöld rose to respond, the mood in the assembly hall was extremely tense. He restated what he had earlier said about impartiality and argued that Khrushchev's proposal for a three-member secretary-general would weaken the office, making it impossible to act effectively. "By resigning, I would, therefore, at the present difficult and dangerous juncture, throw the Organization to the winds. I have no right to do so." At these words, the hall erupted in applause. And when he went on to say "I shall remain in my post, . . ." another wave of applause rolled across the floor. Khrushchev and his colleagues pounded their fists on their desks.

"It is very easy to resign," Hammarskjöld continued. "It is not so easy to stay on. It is very easy to bow to the wish of a big power. It is another matter to resist." As Hammarskjöld concluded, the delegates rose and gave him an ovation that lasted for several minutes. Hammarskjöld seemed embarrassed by this overwhelming show of support. He fidgeted and finally wrote a note to his close aide Ralph Bunche, sitting next to him. "Did I read it all right?" As the demonstration of support continued, Bunche wrote back, "Perfectly. . . . Thus the greatest — and most spontaneous — demonstration in UN annals. Congratulations."

The following evening Khrushchev hosted a party and invited the secretary-general to attend. Hammarskjöld, after confirming that the invitation was genuine, reluctantly attended. Khrushchev welcomed him to the party with a bear hug and told the secretary-general that he should have more Soviets on his staff. Khrushchev later explained to newsmen that his cordiality to Hammarskjöld was in line with an old custom of certain mountain people of the Soviet Union, who treat an enemy well when he is inside their house but feel free to slit his throat once he is outside.

As Khrushchev prepared to return to the Soviet Union he made a farewell speech at the UN. Standing for the last time at the assembly podium, he mentioned that he was "not fighting Mr. Hammarskjöld personally," reminding those gathered that the secretary-general had once been his guest in the Soviet Union. At that time Khrushchev had rowed him in a boat on the Black Sea, but Hammarskjöld had never repaid the favor. When Khrushchev finished his statement, Hammarskjöld replied that he would repay Khrushchev someday because he was sure that the Soviet leader "would discover that I know how to row," pausing significantly before adding, "following only my own compass."

> *A mature man is his own judge. In the end, his only form of support is being faithful to his own convictions. The advice of others may be welcome and valuable, but it does not free him from responsibility.*
> —DAG HAMMARSKJÖLD

9

Heart of Darkness

Nikita Khrushchev's visit to the UN was not the last time Hammarskjöld had to respond to Soviet accusations. Barely two months after the stormy opening session of the UN in September 1960, Patrice Lumumba was captured and murdered by Mobutu's forces in the Congo. Hammarskjöld found himself once again embroiled in the turmoil still raging in the central African nation, facing renewed Soviet demands for his resignation. Hammarskjöld responded to the Soviet Union's insistence that he be replaced with a standing offer of his resignation, which the UN delegates could accept any time they considered it in the best interests of the UN. A vote of confidence was then taken in which the delegates showed their continuing overwhelming approval of the secretary-general.

The Soviet Union found another way to hamper Hammarskjöld's Congo effort. They refused to contribute any money to the UN for that purpose. France followed suit, and it soon became a very serious problem. Hammarskjöld pointed out that the amount of money needed was small. The total cost, he told the UN delegates, of the Congo operation for a whole year was less than the world's bill for armaments for a single day. If the UN pulled out of the Congo, Hammarskjöld warned, that country would soon be torn by civil war, tribal conflicts, and

Do not seek death. Death will find you. But seek the road which makes death a fulfillment.
—DAG HAMMARSKJÖLD

With Prime Minister Cyrille Adoula of the Republic of the Congo, Hammarskjöld stands at attention during the playing of the country's national anthem. Hammarskjöld returned to Africa in September 1961 in a final effort to resolve the Congo crisis.

UNITED NATIONS

Katangese refugees arrive in droves to receive food rations at this UN camp in Elisabethville. While fighting between Katangese and Congolese troops continued, the UN tried to supply the people of both countries with the basic necessities.

political and economic collapse. In those circumstances it would quickly become a battleground for the Cold War nations. The delegates voted for the necessary funds.

Hammarskjöld's efforts to bring order back into the Congo began to pay off in other ways as well. The Congolese leaders, fighting among themselves for several months, finally decided to join together and reunite their torn country. Although they represented only five of the Congo's six states — Katanga still remained independent — their unity would be a giant step toward solving the terrible problems that were plaguing the country at all levels.

In the summer of 1961, as the Congo crisis began to ease, Hammarskjöld welcomed some relief from this year-long nightmare. But another problem immediately arose elsewhere.

Tunisia, in northwestern Africa, faces France, 400 miles away across the Mediterranean Sea. Having wrested their independence from France in 1956, the Tunisians were angry that France continued to maintain a military base at the city of Bizerte. President Habib Bourguiba, aware of his people's resentment of the French presence, had repeatedly requested the evacuation of the base, but President Charles de Gaulle of France refused, claiming the base was necessary for French security. In July 1961 a group of Tunisian soldiers and civilians surrounded the base. The French troops at the base attacked, using fiery napalm bombs as well as conventional weapons. Over 1,000 Tunisians were killed, and about 20 French soldiers died. When French troops occupied Bizerte, the Tunisian government requested help from the UN.

Armed with a Security Council resolution requesting the French to pull back to their base, Hammarskjöld went to Tunisia to begin negotiations. He held discussions with Tunisian leaders, but the French refused to negotiate with him or attend the General Assembly session on Bizerte. Despite Hammarskjöld's discouragement at the lack of cooperation, his personal visit was sincerely welcomed by the Tunisians as an indication to the small nations of the world that the UN would stand up to the major powers for the causes of international law and justice. A second UN resolution, on August 25, supported Tunisia's right to have the French troops removed, and in October the French drew back to the base. Two years later the French completely withdrew from Tunisian soil.

As the Tunisian problem was winding down, an old difficulty was revived in the Congo. The Katanga leaders were still reluctant to bring their state back into the Republic of the Congo. Although most of the Belgians had left, and the Belgian government was finally cooperating with Hammarskjöld, mercenary soldiers from other countries had gone to Katanga to help Moise Tshombe fight for continued independence. Tshombe paid these mercenaries very well.

It was still Hammarskjöld's policy to avoid using the UN troops to force Katanga to rejoin the Congo. Yet he felt that stronger measures were necessary, and he decided to try to force the mercenaries to leave the country. As the situation in Katanga grew more tense, the opposition there to the UN officials and troops increased. Constant criticism, distortions of fact, and false rumors were spread by the

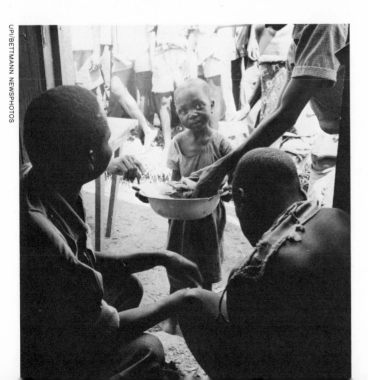

UPI/BETTMANN NEWSPHOTOS

A refugee child patiently awaits food supplied by the UN Food and Agriculture Organization at a hospital in famine-stricken Bakwanga, Congo. The Congolese civil war only exacerbated the country's already disastrous economic problems.

UNITED NATIONS

Hammarskjöld (right) listens to criticism of his policies on the Congo during a Security Council meeting on February 15, 1961. A few member nations, like France and the Soviet Union, were unwilling to contribute more money toward the UN efforts there.

> Never measure the height of a mountain until you have reached the top. Then you will see how low it was.
>
> —DAG HAMMARSKJÖLD

mercenaries, government leaders, and representatives of Western governments. The only bright note was the new spirit of unity in the rest of the Congo, expressed in the government's invitation to Hammarskjöld to visit there. Hammarskjöld decided to use the opportunity to make one final effort to bring Katanga back within the jurisdiction of the Congo government.

Just before he left New York on September 12, 1961, Hammarskjöld told a close friend that this would be his last personal effort to solve the Katanga problem. If he failed, he said, he would resign as secretary-general.

The constant setbacks in the Congo had taken their toll on Hammarskjöld. Working day and night for over a year, enduring verbal onslaughts from not only the Congolese but from all quarters of the globe, Hammarskjöld's tremendous strength and stamina were meeting their severest test. The mountain he had predicted he would have to climb when he took over as secretary-general more than eight years earlier was becoming steeper and more treacherous every day.

When he arrived in Léopoldville, Hammarskjöld was warmly greeted by the Congolese leaders. They told him they were very grateful to him for working so hard to help reestablish the legal government and prevent the country from falling into chaos and civil war. But Hammarskjöld soon heard reports that things were going terribly wrong in Katanga. The UN force there had tried to round up the mercenaries, but it had met with violent resistance. There was fighting in the streets and UN soldiers were being killed. Hammarskjöld was greatly distressed and sent word to the UN representative there to stop the fighting as soon as possible. He had never intended the UN soldiers to engage in open warfare.

During the customary receptions and formal dinners in Léopoldville, Hammarskjöld worried about the situation in Katanga, where the fighting continued. The only military plane belonged to the Katangese, which gave them a great advantage. It strafed and bombed at will. Knowing that if he could not be found by UN officials a cease-fire could not be arranged, Tshombe, the Katangese leader, played hide-and-seek.

Hammarskjöld decided he would have to contact Tshombe and arrange to meet him personally. He was convinced that if he could talk with Tshombe he could persuade him to meet with the Congolese leaders. Such a meeting would open the way for finally reuniting all the states of the Congo.

Hammarskjöld sent a message to Tshombe asking for an immediate and unconditional cease-fire and

Hammarskjöld arrives at Léopoldville on September 13, 1961, to meet with Adoula and Mobutu (in uniform, at left) for discussion on UN support to the Congo. By this time, all of the Congolese provinces had reunited except for Katanga, which remained independent.

a meeting in northern Rhodesia (now the nation of Zambia), a few miles beyond the Katanga border. Tshombe sent a guarded reply but agreed to meet Hammarskjöld as he requested, and the secretary-general left immediately for the rendezvous.

Hammarskjöld boarded a UN plane with a few UN officials and a small crew. In the late afternoon of September 17, he left the Congo on the seven-hour flight to meet Tshombe. What happened at the end of that flight will probably never be known.

Everything seemed to go normally until the plane approached the airfield. During the flight Hammarskjöld worked on his translation of a book by German Jewish philosopher Martin Buber. As the plane prepared for landing just after midnight, the pilot radioed the control tower that he could see the airfield lights and would land in a few minutes.

A short time later those waiting on the ground saw the plane fly over at about 2,000 feet. But the plane never returned. Ten miles away the plane cut a curving swath through the trees, apparently as it was turning to prepare to land. The left wingtip touched first and the plane cartwheeled before breaking apart and bursting into flame.

All but one of the 16 persons on board were burned in the flames. Hammarskjöld, who disliked wearing a seatbelt, was thrown clear. He died of multiple internal injuries a few moments after the crash. He was found lying on his back, a peaceful

UN peacekeeping soldiers in the Congo are pinned down behind an armored personnel carrier by Katangese gunfire. Hammarskjöld was convinced peace was coming to the Congo, but he would not live to see Katanga reunited with the rest of the country.

UNITED NATIONS

UPI/BETTMANN NEWSPHOTOS

look on his face, one hand holding a clump of grass.

Many people charged that Hammarskjöld had been deliberately killed. Numerous theories, mostly unrealistic, filled newspapers for many weeks, and several articles and books were written on the subject. The UN and the Swedish government carefully investigated the crash but found no strong evidence to support any one theory. The possible causes were attack from ground or air, sabotage, human error, or mechanical failure. The evidence showed only that the plane had hit the treetops in an area of rising elevation.

The world was stunned. Tshombe, appearing upset by the disaster, placed a wreath on Hammarskjöld's coffin before it was sent to Sweden. Two days after the crash, he signed a cease-fire agreement with the UN. Hammarskjöld's other main objective in the Congo took longer to achieve. The state of Katanga finally rejoined the Congo 14 months later, in January 1963. The subsequent experience of other newly independent African nations showed that Hammarskjöld's work in the Congo had clearly

Wreckage of the airplane that crashed in northern Rhodesia (now Zambia) on September 18, 1961, killing all aboard, including Hammarskjöld, who had been traveling to meet with Tshombe to negotiate a cease-fire between the forces of the Congo and Katanga.

105

helped to stabilize and strengthen that country. Congo President Mobutu, speaking at the UN nine years after Hammarskjöld's death, proclaimed the UN Congo operation a success: "The Democratic Republic of the Congo is a living testimony to what the United Nations Organization is capable of when it is given the appropriate means." In 1971 the Congo, including Katanga, became the Republic of Zaire.

All of Sweden was in mourning as Hammarskjöld's coffin arrived by plane. A huge torchlight parade filled the center of Stockholm, the capital city, and the following day the funeral was held in Hammarskjöld's boyhood home, Uppsala.

The king and queen of Sweden led many representatives from all over the world in paying their last respects to Hammarskjöld at the great Uppsala cathedral. After the service in the cathedral, the coffin was put on an open gun carriage, until then used only for royal funerals. A long procession of people followed the carriage to the cemetery near the university, where the coffin was buried in the Hammarskjöld family plot.

Four weeks later, the Nobel Peace Prize was

A long procession, including family members, the king and queen of Sweden, and prominent world figures, follows the pallbearers carrying the body of Hammarskjöld to burial on September 29, 1961, in Uppsala, Sweden.

awarded to Hammarskjöld. In November, a new UN building, housing the library, was completed. Dedicated to the fallen secretary-general, it was named the Dag Hammarskjöld Library.

Hammarskjöld believed that his highest duty was to serve his fellow human beings. As secretary-general of the United Nations, he drew a map of high accomplishment that his successors would strive to follow. For eight and a half years, through a combination of personal diplomacy, courage, and hard work, Hammarskjöld greatly enlarged the power and influence of the UN. In bringing a new level of respect to the organization, he defused many explosive situations. Hammarskjöld created a strong leadership role for an international organization that had to depend on the support of many diverse, often antagonistic, nations. He showed a genius for forging an effective and forceful policy of international peace and cooperation from this diverse group. This intensely private man, largely unknown outside his own country in 1953, gave himself to the world and became in just a few years one of the most admired leaders of the 20th century.

A crowd solemnly watches as Hammarskjöld's casket is lowered into the family grave. In less than a decade, from 1953 to 1961, the quiet Swedish diplomat had earned the world's respect and gratitude. His dedication to peace left a lasting mark on the United Nations.

Further Reading

Goodrich, Leland M. *The United Nations in a Changing World.* New York: Columbia University Press, 1974.

Hammarskjöld, Dag. *Markings.* Translated by Leif Sjoberg and W. H. Auden. New York: Alfred A. Knopf, 1964.

———. *Servant of Peace: A Selection of the Speeches and Statements of Dag Hammarskjöld.* Edited by Wilder Foote. New York: Harper & Row, 1963.

Hoskyns, Catherine. *The Congo Since Independence—January 1960 to December 1961.* Oxford: Royal Institute of International Affairs, 1965.

Lash, Joseph P. *Hammarskjöld: Custodian of the Brushfire Peace.* Garden City, N.Y.: Doubleday & Co., 1961.

Soderberg, Sten. *Hammarskjöld: A Pictorial Biography.* New York: The Viking Press, 1962.

Urquhart, Brian. *Hammarskjöld.* New York: Alfred A. Knopf, 1972.

Chronology

July 29, 1905	Born Dag Hjalmar Hammarskjöld in Jönköping, Sweden
1925	Receives his B.A. degree in literature and philosophy
1933	Earns doctorate in economics
1936	Appointed undersecretary of Swedish Finance Ministry
1940	Norway falls to the German army; Sweden remains officially neutral
1941	Hammarskjöld is appointed chairman of the Bank of Sweden; works to provide secret financial assistance to the Norwegian government-in-exile
1947	Serves as a delegate to the Marshall Plan economic conferences in Paris
1948	Named chief Swedish delegate to the Organization for European Economic Cooperation (OEEC)
1949	Appointed cabinet secretary in the Swedish Ministry of Foreign Affairs
1950	Becomes president of the OEEC
1951	Serves as vice-minister of foreign affairs and a member of the Swedish cabinet
1952	Swedish planes are shot down by Soviet Union; Hammarskjöld defuses the crisis
March 31, 1953	Hammarskjöld is elected secretary-general of the United Nations
1954	Elected to the Swedish Academy, which awards the Nobel Prizes
Jan. 1955	Visits China to confer with Zhou Enlai; six months later, the Chinese government releases captured American airmen
1956	Negotiates a Middle East cease-fire Suez crisis and deployment of first UN peacekeeping force Soviet Union invades Hungary
Sept. 1957	Hammarskjöld is reelected UN secretary-general
1958	Lebanon crisis
1959	Hammarskjöld visits Nikita Khrushchev in the Soviet Union Sends technical assistance to Laos
1960	Thirteen newly independent African nations are admitted to the UN
July 1960	Congo crisis begins
Aug. 1960	Hammarskjöld leads UN troops into Katanga, Congo
Sept.–Oct. 1960	Confrontation with Khrushchev at the UN
Sept. 18, 1961	Killed in plane crash in northern Rhodesia (now Zambia)

Index

Richard N. Sheldon is Assistant Director of the Publications Program of the National Historical Publications and Records Commission in Washington, D.C. He has taught history at Rollins College, the University of Maryland, Montgomery College, and George Mason University.

Arthur M. Schlesinger, jr., taught history at Harvard for many years and is currently Albert Schweitzer Professor of the Humanities at City University of New York. He is the author of numerous highly praised works in American history and has twice been awarded the Pulitzer Prize. He served in the White House as special assistant to Presidents Kennedy and Johnson.